Allegory in Stone:
A Short Study of the Shakespeare Monument

M. R. Osborne, M.A.

M. R. Osborne is a practicing lawyer, independent researcher and author. His Bachelors and Masters degrees were in Theology at the University of Birmingham, England.

At various times in his career he has written papers on both legal and esoteric subjects. A member of the Societas Rosicruciana in Anglia (S.R.I.A.) he was awarded the prestigious Companion of Christian Rosenkreutz award in 2017 for his paper on Martinez de Pasqually.

His most recent books are *The Lessons of Lyons* (2021), *The Most Holy Trinosophia – A Book of the Dead* (2021) and *The Brazen Serpent: Order and Chaos* (2022).

Rose Circle Publications
P.O. Box 854
Bayonne, NJ 07002, U.S.A.
www.rosecirclebooks.com

Contents

	Preface	7
	Introduction	15
1	The Threefold Wisdom	25
2	Utopia	37
3	Stay, Passenger	43
4	Freemasonry?	47
5	The Kaballah	63
6	The Ciphers	81
7	Kether, the Crown	91
8	Rosicrucianism	95
10	Concluding Remarks	103
	Selected Bibliography	107
	Index	109
	References	111

Preface

The mystery surrounding the occult influences that shaped William Shakespeare's art have long been a source of fascination for me. This interest was not extinguished by the interminable literature classes at school and college but persevered for more personal reasons. The most notable of which is my probable descent from Richard Shakespeare, my fourteenth great-grandfather.

For the interested reader, the connection comes about thus. My five-times great-grandfather, John Shakespeare, a sadler of St. Mary's Warwick, married Sarah Hastelow of Aston Cantlow near the recusant estate of Wootton Wawen. Their daughter Winifred, my four times great-grandmother was born in 1789, and lived to an advanced age, passing down the story of her father's descent from the Shakespeares of Snitterfield. Contrary to some erroneous research, Richard Shakespeare (1490-1561) bore five sons. As is well documented, he relocated his family from Wroxhall to Snitterfield. His third son, Thomas Shakespeare, my thirteenth great-grandfather, settled in nearby Rowington. There followed six generations in Rowington. until John Shakespeare (1693-1752) moved three miles to Hatton. It was here that Winifred's father was born, and whose subsequent move to Warwick - where his sibling James was apprenticed a tanner - was in furtherance of gainful work.

That there is befuddlement on the part of Shakespeare genealogists as to Richard Shakespeare's descendants does not in the least surprise me, since Roman Catholic baptismal records were usually made in the private chapels of the landed Catholic estates of

Warwickshire, such as Baddesley Clinton, Wootton Wawen, Grove Park and so forth. This was also the case with Winifred. The progress of the Shakespeares of Rowington to the outlying villages and estates about Snitterfield mirrors the fate of many husbandmen of the period. The circumambulation of the Rowington branch was necessitated by large families and the rise of enclosures, then tearing apart the old agrarian order in England.

This makes William Shakespeare my first cousin thirteen times removed. This is of no particular interest to anyone other than myself, save for the debate surrounding Shakespeare's purported Catholicism. For my part, I can state that the Shakespeares of St. Mary's were Catholic. Were that connection to be confirmed in the case of the Stratford branch, once and for all, then it would cast a strategic light on Shakespeare's outlook, his motivation and the sources of inspiration which engendered his brilliance, and which may at times have come at the cost of his conscience.

The second reason for my interest – that which led to this short book – arises from my Christian mysticism. I am a Rosicrucian and my own esoteric leanings, particularly in Christian Martinism, have provided me down the years with a sound grounding for the task of penetrating certain of the mysteries which permeate Shakespeare's funerary monument.

I must confess another, third, motive for the present work: it is one which lies in a series of lucid dreams from several years ago. Dreams are acknowledged throughout the Secret Tradition as a powerful means by which we recharge our minds and bodies. Dreams are, and always have been, a source of healing and insight, not only to the mystic, but to anyone seeking to master the raw, unmanifest aspect of our subconscious. It is a fact that dreams speak directly and powerfully to people's basic spiritual concerns, and there is good reason to theorise that the very nature of spirit may equate with our psyche.

According to Carl Jung, the collective unconscious is common to all human beings, and is responsible amongst other things for our spirituality, having been inherited from humanity's past, collective experiences. An inherited ancestral memory, perhaps even evidence of a group soul. Thus, Jung wrote that dreams may indicate the existence of this background activity. Though we may not understand what the thoughts and images in the collective unconscious are, he taught that the psyche could tap into it. Indeed, he also addressed the issue of an afterlife, which, if it exists, equates the psyche with the immortal soul, as it requires neither space nor time to exist.

In my dreams I experienced *indirect* encounters (for want of a better word) with the presence of Shakespeare summoning me from beyond the other side of a closed entrance to his tomb. Obviously, I am not describing Shakespeare's actual grave, which is neither in a crypt nor tomb, and which bears absolutely no resemblance to the idealized place of my dream. Regarding these dreams I wish to say nothing further, other than I have always interpreted them as a message from the unconscious to tell this story. Well, it has taken me a long time to finally start writing, and now that I have, I seem to find myself pouring out ideas and books at remarkable rapidity – which reflects that these ideas have been written over a hundred times in my mind these past fifty years. I am now the same age as Shakespeare when he died, so if not write now, then when? We must all, if we can, exchange the sceptre for the trowel, and start working on something that will survive us. To that end, this book is dedicated to you.

M. R. Osborne, M.A.
Northampton, April 2022

Shakespeare's funerary monument on the north wall of the chancel at Holy Trinity Church, Stratford-upon-Avon

TO THE MEMORIE
of the deceased Authour Maister
W. S H A K E S P E A R E.

Shake-speare, at length thy pious fellowes give
The world thy Workes : thy Workes, by which, out-live
Thy Tombe, thy name must when that stone is rent,
This monument cannot be overthrown,
And Time dissolves thy Stratford Moniment,
When Wilton lies low, level'd with the ground
Here we alive shall view thee still. This Booke,
By this (great Lady) thou must then be known
When Brasse and Marble fade, shall make thee looke
Where, in eternal Brass remains thy Name.
Fresh to all Ages : when Posteritie
Unto thy voice Eternity hath given
Shall loath what's new, thinke all is prodegie
That is not Shake-speares; ev'ry Line, each Verse
Here shall revive, redeeme thee from thy Herse.
Nor Fire, nor cankring Age, as Naso said,
Of his, thy wit-fraught Booke shall once invade.
Nor shall I e're beleeve, or thinke thee dead.
(Though mist) untill our bankrout Stage be sped
(Imposible) with some new straine t'out-do
Passions of Juliet, and her Romeo ;
Or till I heare a Scene more nobly take,
Then when thy half-Sword parlying Romans spake.
Till these, till any of thy Volumes rest
Shall with more fire, more feeling be exprest,
Be sure, our Shake-speare, thou canst never dye,
But crown'd with Lawrell, live eternally.

Leonard Digges, 1623

Introduction

Not long after William Shakespeare's death on 23 April 1616, a cantilevered monument was erected to his memory on the northeast wall of the chancel at Holy Trinity Church, Stratford-upon-Avon. We know this because the prologue to the First Folio in 1623 (above) by Leonard Digges refers to it.

An interesting fact about the Digges family, as noted by Keith Browning in his book *Shakespeare Reinvented*,[i] is that Leonard's father the geometrician and astronomer Thomas Digges, had been educated by John Dee (1527-1608). Dee was the most notable occultist in the court of Elizabeth I. That Digges appreciated Shakespeare personally is beyond doubt, as Browning points out there exists a contemporaneous note on the flyleaf of a book of Spanish poetry in which Shakespeare is noted by Digges as the greater poet.[ii] We therefore have an intriguing and contemporary connection between Shakespeare and the Digges family.

The Stratford monument is made from a wide array of materials, but again, this is not uncommon for the period. The limestone figure of Shakespeare (since whitewashed, then repainted) holds a quill and a blank page of paper resting on a cushion. There are two Corinthian columns made of black polished marble, and the inlaid panels are of black touchstone. The capitals, bases and skull are carved sandstone. The two sandstone putti[iii] or cherubim represent labour (holding a trowel to symbolise "Adam's toil" tilling the earth), and death (holding an inverted luminary or torch – mirroring the blank page wrought by obliteration). The architraves, frieze and cornice were originally made from red-veined white alabaster (but replaced with white marble in

1749). Shakespeare's family coat of arms rests between the putti. Of particular and immediate interest to the casually passing Freemason are the two pillars, trowel, inverted torch and skull, which we will touch upon in more detail later. The Masonic reader will also take note that not only is the monument mounted on the north wall, but it is also in fact placed on the north-east wall of the building.

On one hand, the Shakespeare monument is a typical memorial for a notable individual of the period, as can be seen from the example below of the kneeling effigy monument of Sir Robert Leigh in Chingford parish church, erected in 1612. Indeed, by the time of his death Shakespeare was the leading grandee in the town of Stratford, he owned New Place, its best house, and was unquestioningly granted the honour of being buried in the chancel in front of the High Altar, in his capacity as a lay rector. On the other hand, it is markedly different in its inclusion of clever ciphers and gematrical codes.

Sir Robert Leigh, 1612

There is no record to show who paid for the monument, and some have posited the wealthy benefactor of the arts

Lady Anne Clifford (1590 – 1676). This is unlikely because the quality of the carving is said to be sub-par. Writing for the Church Monuments Society in 2010, Adam White says:

> "The sculpture has all the hallmarks of the 'Southwark School' of foreign craftsmen who settled south of the river Thames during the sixteenth century to avoid a ban on immigrant labour which was imposed by the City of London livery companies. They developed a distinctive style which was adapted from work in the Netherlands from which they came, using a colourful combination of materials, particularly alabaster and black marble, enhanced with a great deal of paint and gilding and a bastardised style of classical architecture for the surrounds. The herald and antiquary Sir William Dugdale noted in his diary for 1653 that this memorial and that of John Combe nearby were the work of 'one Gerard Johnson'. Dugdale is not an entirely reliable source in such matters but his testimony must bear some weight and it points to Gerard Johnson the Younger, a second-generation member of one of the leading Southwark workshops ... The inscription does not cohere with the monument itself. It is a scrappy assemblage of words, crudely cut, the lettering being far below the standard of most Southwark work."[iv]

The Shakespeare monument is a curious example of Jacobean geometric and sacred ciphers, no doubt commissioned by those "pious fellows" (in pejorative terms his "fans") who knew Shakespeare and shared his occult interests. It is quite possible Shakespeare may have commissioned the monument himself, which was common practice. However, by all accounts he died suddenly from unknown causes not long after a heavy drinking session with Ben Jonson. It is said that if Shakespeare did commission the monument during his lifetime then:

> "[as] a work of routine commercial art [it] bears no imprint of a superior artistic imagination. Shakespeare did not even select the best of the available London carvers."[v]

Francis Bacon and the "Two Shakespeares"

This work is not the first, nor will it be the last, observation of the "hidden" Rosicrucian symbolism contained in the Shakespeare monument at Holy Trinity Church. One interesting and comparatively recent attempt to interpret the monument as evidence of "two Shakespeares" (one the actor from Stratford, the other the esteemed luminary Sir Francis Bacon) was undertaken by Peter Dawkins for the Francis Bacon Research Trust in 2018 (updated in 2020).[vi] It struck me that the central tenet of his argument for interpreting the monument as a cunningly concealed attribute to Bacon was the crucial phrase "whose name, doth deck y^s tombe, far more, then cost" and numerological principles applied to the Latin epitaph. This was the Baconian smoking gun. My research into my own family tree revealed, however, an exceptionally strong *Roman Catholic* loyalty amongst the Shakespeares, which persisted until well into the early nineteenth century. The great "cost" was explainable, to me at least, as a reference to the suppression of the poet's Catholicism in his writings (assuming the Snitterfield and Stratford branches were likewise Catholics).

The Dawkins paper is nonetheless correct in its assertion that the monument "is a major gateway into the mystery of Shakespeare."[vii] It does, however, make several erroneous assumptions about the Freemasonic, Hermetic and Kabbalistic influences that may be present in the monument. Their paper lacks a precise understanding of the esoteric substance and a detailed, working understanding of those traditions. It is no good to just dabble about the edges of esoteric Freemasonry in all its diverse forms when considering ciphers and symbols. It is one thing to cite them, quite another to deliberate upon them enough to convincingly determine whether it was Bacon or Shakespeare who wrote the plays, and to conclude that is why the page is left blank on a stone memorial. It is far more likely that the "great mystery" or secret is Shakespeare's Catholicism, and it need hardly be pointed out that membership of Christian esoteric orders were tolerated by Roman Catholicism until the late eighteenth century.

The monument can only have been raised with the consent of Shakespeare's widow and family, who either paid for its erection themselves, or who permitted his friends to do so. It is inconceivable that his family had no involvement with the monument, no matter how strained the relationships. It might however explain why it was not the costliest, notwithstanding that Shakespeare died one of the richest in Stratford. We know from the First Folio that the memorial was raised prior to 1623, although whether it existed in its current form is less certain. Peter Dawkins provides a very helpful history of the monument's restoration and concludes that it is essentially unchanged save for the replacement of the red and white alabaster architraves with plain white marble,[viii] aesthetically completing the superstructure of the entablature. Even the cushion replacing a woolsack is discounted, notwithstanding its appearance in the several engravings of the monument. In other words the restoration was sympathetic. In her 1999 essay Clark J. Holloway noted:

"Although the first reference to Shakespeare's monument is in 1623, the first engraving depicting the monument was published in 1656 in Sir William Dugdale's *Antiquities of Warwickshire Illustrated: from Records, Leiger-Books, Manuscripts, Charters, Evidences, Tombs, and Arms: Beautified with Maps, Prospects and Portraitures*. Although the engraving in Dugdale's *Antiquities*, executed by Wenceslaus Hollar or his assistant Richard Gaywood from a sketch made by Dugdale in 1634, has the distinction of being the first depiction of Shakespeare's monument, it is hardly a faithful rendering. Among the numerous errors in the engraving, the absence of the pen and paper held by Shakespeare in the monument we see today and the bulky rendering of the cushion on which Shakespeare rests his arms are seen as the "smoking gun" in the anti-Stratfordian argument that the monument has been altered some time after its creation as a part of the "conspiracy" to fool people into believing that the illiterate boor from Stratford actually wrote the works attributed to William Shakespeare."[ix]

The various sketches and engravings are pictured here, of which only Charles Grignion's version postdates the restoration of 1749:

Dugdale's sketch, 1634

Hollar, 1656

Rowe, 1709

Vertue, 1723

Grignion, 1786

The first photograph taken of the monument, 1863

The chancel as it appeared in 1723

As for the columns, Dawkins equates these with the Roman Pantheon, a rotunda, and assumes an intended parallel with Shakespeare's Globe Theatre.[x] This is a highly imaginative and fanciful analogy. There is nothing circular about the monument, save for its reduction by geometric principles detailed later in this book, and the use of Corinthian columns in the monument was not an attempt to mimic the Pantheon, which has plain Tuscan pillars. The two columns do, however, have very profound esoteric significance, as we shall note later. For now, it is sufficient to note that the monument does indeed resemble a temple or shrine, its intended meaning.

Chapter One:
The Threefold Wisdom

The inscriptions on the black touchstone are of the utmost importance to our present investigation. The first inscription is in Latin, the second is a poem in English.

The Latin text reads:

IUDICIO PYLIUM, GENIO SOCRATEM, ARTE MARONEM,
TERRA TEGIT, POPVLVS MÆRET, OLYMPVS HABET

This translates as:

A PYLIAN IN JUDGEMENT, A SOCRATES IN GENIUS, A MARO IN ART,
THE EARTH BURIES HIM, THE PEOPLE MOURN, OLYMPUS POSSESSES HIM

The poem in English below the Latin inscription reads:

STAY PASSENGER, WHY GOEST THOV BY SO FAST,
READ IF THOV CANST, WHOM ENVIOVS DEATH HATH PLAST

WITH IN THIS MONVMENT SHAKSPEARE: WITH WHOME,
QVICK NATVRE DIDE: WHOSE NAME, DOTH DECK Y^S TOMBE,
FAR MORE, THEN COST: SIEH ALL, Y^T HE HATH WRITT,
LEAVES LIVING ART, BVT PAGE, TO SERVE HIS WITT.

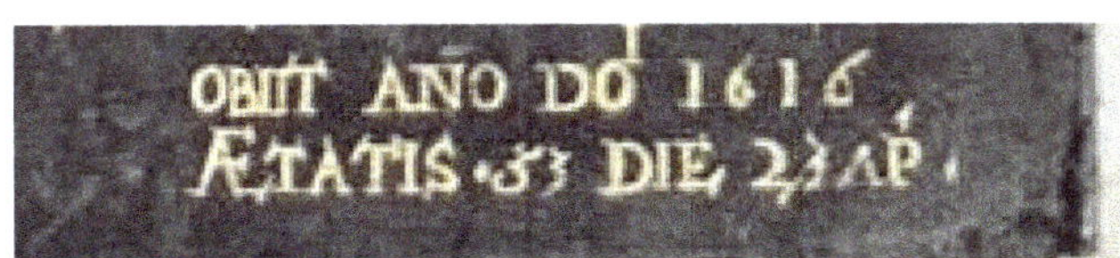

Just below the poem is the following text:

OBIT ANO
DO 1616
AETATIS-53 DIE 23 APR

The abbreviated words at the foot of the inscription advise us of the age and year of Shakespeare's death. It tells us he died aged 53, on 23 April, 1616.

Judicio Pylium - Nestor of Pylos

In the Latin inscription, the impression given is that Shakespeare is being likened to the wise king of Pylos, Nestor. This references the character in Homer's epic poems the *Iliad* and the *Odyssey*. In the *Iliad,* Nestor provides more ships for the campaign against Troy than any other of king Agamemnon's allies, and acts as his most trusted counsellor (the "old war horse"). It is Nestor who attempts a diplomatic solution to the war, and whose counsel was followed with an embassy of the Greeks to king Priam. Nestor and Odysseus also invent a signaling system for the Greek ships to coordinate their attacks once this peace embassy is rejected, and it is he who mediates between the fiery Agamemnon and Achilles when they quarrel:

> "Nestor rose between them,
> The man of winning words, the dear
> Speaker of Pylos.
> Sweeter than honey from his tongue the
> Voice flowed on and on"
> *Illiad,* Book 1, 290-292

Nestor of Pylos

Zeus even sends a false dream to Agamemnon in the form of Nestor, an act of trickery which leads to the near defeat of the Greek forces when they were pushed back to their ships by the Trojans. It is Nestor who persuades the Greeks to continue fighting, and who ultimately encourages Achilles back into the fray. Agamemnon held Nestor in such high esteem that he eulogizes him as follows:

> "Old war-horse,
> If only your knees could match the spirit in
> Your chest
> And your body's strength were played firm
> As rock,
> But the great leveller age, has worn you
> Down.
> If only some other fighter had your years
> And you could march the younger, fitter men."
> *Iliad*, Book 4, 360-365

In the *Odyssey,* Nestor's attributes also include being a good horseman and piety. When Telemachus and Mentor arrive in Pylos, they find Nestor sacrificing dozens of bulls to honour his father, the god Poseidon.[xi]

Socrates by Pietro Bellotti

Shakespeare also appears to be likened to the ancient Greek philosopher Socrates of Athens (470-399 BC), whose elenctic dialogues were posthumously recalled in classical literature. This was the "Socratic Method" of discourse, and influenced Plato himself. It is possible that Shakespeare's admirers were alluding to a form of observational skill on the Poet's part, whereby arguments or hypotheses were cross-examined and placed under a high degree of scrutiny by him. This appears to suggest that Shakespeare may have been circumspect, and did not rush into hasty judgements in debate with acquaintances and critics. Thus, Socrates' questioning method and the ability to consider multiple perspectives is what is probably being alluded to.

There is also an element of the quality of altruism, since Socrates was understood to have taken the time to teach other people his methods. In a sense, this is a continuation of the wisdom of Nestor, as it alludes to the attribution of the dual qualities of wisdom (judgment) and balance (genius).

"A plague of opinion! A man may wear it on both sides, like a leather jerkin."
Thersites, *Troilus and Cressida Act III, Scene 3*

Virgil

Arte Maronem - Virgil of Rome

Maro is a reference to the preeminent Roman poet, Virgil (Publius Vergillus Maro, 70 – 19 BC). Shakespeare probably attended King's New School in Stratford, and if so would have become familiar with Virgil's works and in particular the *Aeneid*.

The interesting point about the *Aeneid* is that, like the *Odyssey*, it is an epic 'sequel' to the *Iliad*, recounting the events that followed Troy's defeat. The story follows events from the perspective of the human-god hybrid Aeneas, the son of Aphrodite and the Trojan prince Anchises, whose motley band of survivors arrived in Italy, and were regarded by the Romans as their founding fathers.

As for Shakespeare, the focus of his interest in Virgil appears to be found in three stories from the *Aeneid*: the tragedy of Queen Dido of Carthage, the sack of Troy, and Aeneas' visit to the Underworld (the latter being the inspiration for Dante's epic poem, the *Divina Comedia*). Thus, the *Aeneid* served as an inspiration for the plots in several of Shakespeare's greatest plays: such as *Hamlet, Macbeth*, and his final and most esoteric manuscript, *The Tempest.*

Aeneas spurned Dido, a plot device that is mentioned no less than four times in *The Tempest*, as well as in *Titus Andronicus, The Merchant of Venice, Henry VI Part II, Antony and Cleopatra, Hamlet*, and *Romeo and Juliet.* One interesting aspect of the story is that Aeneas meets Dido again in the Underworld:

> "Not far from here, outspread on every side, are shown the Mourning Fields; such is the name they bear. Here those whom stern Love has consumed with cruel wasting are hidden in walks withdrawn, embowered in a myrtle grove; even in death the pangs leave them not. In this region he sees Phaedra and Procris, and sad Eriphyle, pointing to the wounds her cruel son had dealt, and Evadne and Pasiphaë. With them goes Laodamia, and Caeneus, once a youth, now a woman, and again turned back by Fate into her form of old. Among them, with wound still fresh, Phoenician Dido was wandering in the great forest, and soon as the Trojan hero stood near and knew her, a dim form amid the shadows – even as, in the early month, one sees or fancies he has seen the moon rise amid the clouds – he shed tears, and spoke to her in tender love:

> "Unhappy Dido! Was the tale true then that came to me, that you were dead and had sought your doom with the sword? Was I, alas! the cause of your death? By the stars I swear, by the world above, and whatever is sacred in the grave below, unwillingly, queen, I parted from your shores. But the gods' decrees, which now constrain me to pass through these shades, through lands squalid and forsaken, and through abysmal night, drove me

with their behests; nor could I deem my going thence would bring on you distress so deep. Stay your step and withdraw not from our view. Whom do you flee? This is the last word Fate suffers me to say to you.

"With these words amid springing tears Aeneas strove to soothe the wrath of the fiery, fierce-eyed queen. She, turning away, kept her looks fixed on the ground and no more changes her countenance as he essays to speak than if she were set in hard flint or Marpesian rock. At length she flung herself away and, still his foe, fled back to the shady grove, where Sychaeus, her lord of former days, responds to her sorrows and gives her love for love. Yet none the less, stricken by her unjust doom, Aeneas attends her with tears afar and pities her as she goes." *Aeneid*, Book VI, 440

Dido, Queen of Carthage

On the basis that Shakespeare was fascinated with the theme of unrequited love, Aeneas's encounter with Dido in Hades is all the more interesting, given the description on his own monument that "Earth buries him." The death of Aeneas introduces the theme of immortality in the hereafter, since his mother the goddess Aphrodite petitions Zeus for her son to be made immortal. Aeneas then becomes known as Jupiter-Indiges. A possible inference to this may be contained in the epitaph's words "Olympus possesses him." Thus, it is possible that the epitaph infers that Shakespeare has all the attributes of a divine-human hybrid in likening him to Nestor and Aeneas.

In *Troilus and Cressida,* written around 1602, Shakespeare builds his entire plot around events of the Trojan War. suspiciously as if the Latin verse on Shakespeare's tomb is directly referencing the *Iliad* as a favourite of his. In the play, Troilus, the youngest son of king Priam, is in love with Cressida, the daughter of a Trojan aristocrat. In a sense he is playing Dido, in a role reversal. Cressida is exchanged with the Greeks in a hostage swap, and falls in love with a Greek, thereby enraging Troilus. The cunning Agamemnon meanwhile continues to plot the course of the war. Achilles is insulted by Agamemnon's hubris, and both Ulysses and Nestor endeavor to reconcile him and, when they do, the Trojan hero Hector is killed by Achilles, and the play ends with the spurned Troilus insulting Cressida's uncle: "Hence, broker-lackey! ignomy and shame: Pursue thy life, and live aye with thy name!." On the surface of things, there is not much to add, but in Act 1 scene 3, Ulysses also praises Nestor:

> "And thou most reverend for thy stretch'd-out life
> I give to both your speeches, which were such As
> Agamemnon and the hand of Greece
> Should hold up high in brass, and such again
> As venerable Nestor, hatch'd in silver,
> Should with a bond of air, strong as the axle-tree
> On which heaven rides, knit all the Greekish ears

To his experienced tongue, yet let it please both,
Thou great, and wise, to hear Ulysses speak."
(Ulysses (to Nestor)

Thus, we may perhaps think of Nestor's wisdom as akin to gamesmanship or tactical insight, which makes a lot of sense if we apply it to Socrates and the methodology he devised. This may reference Shakespeare's head for business and how he rose to become the wealthiest man in Stratford on the back of his career in theatre as well as literary genius. In short, the Latin verse is describing him as an exceptional "all-rounder" when it references the guiding luminaries Nestor, Socrates and Virgil. The meaning is hidden in plain sight, as an inference to the brilliance of Shakespeare and to the dramatic device used in many of his plays.

Chapter Two:
Utopia

The Latin words TERRA TEGIT, POPVLVS MÆRET, OLYMPVS HABET (earth buries him, the people mourn, Olympus possesses him) mirror the preceding three-fold references to Nestor, Socrates and Virgil. This reflects a repeated threefold symbology in the monument. We will consider the most likely meanings of the ciphers within the epitaphs later.

For now, let us note the correspondences in the triple content of the first and second lines, thus:

If we accept the dual correspondences within the monument and its threefold symbolism, then the Latin sentences make more sense expressed as follows:

TERRA TEGIT JUDICIO PYLIUM	POPULUS MÆRET GENIO SOCRATEM	OLYMPUS HABET ARTE MARONEM
THE EARTH BURIES A PYLIAN IN JUDGEMENT	THE PEOPLE MOURN A SOCRATES IN GENIUS	OLYMPUS POSSESSES A MARO IN ART

The Earth Buries a Pylian in Judgement

The theme of a wise man being entombed is a reflection on the mortal nature of humanity. The stories of Nestor's wisdom and noble attributes are well remembered by history; whereas the man Nestor was mortal and died. Homer ties Nestor's age to his wisdom and integrity. Telemachus says of him:

> "we went to Pylos and to Nestor, the shepherd of the people, and he received me in his lofty house and gave me kindly welcome, as a father might his own son who after a long time had newly come from afar: even so kindly he tended me with his glorious sons." *Odyssey*, Book 17

These words, read in combination, are not likening Shakespeare to Nestor (at his passing he was far from old), but are a meditation on the course of wisdom being brought to an end by death. They are also an indirect reflection on the parting of the physical aspect of man and his mind, or intellect.

The reference to the internment of wisdom is reminiscent of the legendry burial chamber of Christian Rosenkreutz, whose tomb recalled the alchemical Quest for the Philosopher's Stone: *Visita Interiora Terrae Rectificando Invenies Occultum Lapidem* ("Visit the Interior Parts of the Earth; by Rectification Thou Shalt Find the Hidden Stone").

The People Mourn a Socrates in Genius

It is likely that the judgement (wisdom) of Nestor, the intellect of of Socrates and the creativity of Virgil are a play on the governance of Plato's Utopia, the ideal society. In his *Republic,* there is a series of dialogues between Plato, Socrates, and an unidentified third person in a way that engages the reader in much the same way as the English poem on Shakespeare's monument does. This is not coincidental, and both the Latin and English verses are a microcosm of the *Republic*, a sort of "pocketbook guide" to the convictions of the Rosicrucians.

This comes about because Socrates's death marked the failure of the Greek state to co-exist with genius and free thought. The *Republic* debates what justice is and explains that, until one knows, it is impossible to see it as a virtue. Author Daniel Tutt states:

> "It is important to note the context of the cosmology of the Greeks at the time. Their view of the human condition was such that there is no possible change to the material conditions in life. Men are born throughout the centuries to a natural or historical spectacle that essentially always stays the same. Indeed, in Greek times, freedom relied on being in the presence of one's peers. This is how all citizenship was developed, out of dialogue and deliberation."[xii]

The purpose of the epitaphs on the monument is to highlight imbalance between the ideal (above) and the reality (below). Without toleration of free thought, creativity and progress are permanently stymied. Obviously, this was a radical outlook in Shakespeare's time too, where Catholicism and non-conformism was not tolerated. The verses are therefore highly suggestive of the Rosicrucian desire to create Utopia, but in a way that has more of a political than esoteric feel about it.

Plato was a student of Socrates, and sought to break the rigid Greek view of the citizen. Whilst Plato's *Republic* was not democratic and still favoured a class system, it was nonetheless a meritocracy. The ruling elite were "the golden ones" or philosopher class. The general idea was that science and education would eliminate poverty and warfare. As Keith Browning states:

> "Plato's 'golden ones' were to be the ultimate product of a 50 year education program, creating an elite group of 'philosopher-kings', who would re-organise the world and in so doing,. The 'golden ones' were an obvious template for the Rosicrucians, who came to regard themselves as the intellectual elite of the scientific world."[xiii]

It was the task of the Rosicrucians, the highly secretive Brotherhood of the Rosy Cross, to change things. This mysterious group first announced their existence in 1614 with the publication in Germany of a manifesto known as the *Fama Fraternitatus*. It is possible the pamphlet existed prior to 1614, as a notary to the Archduke Maximilian of Kessel, Adam Haselmeyer, is said to have read it as early as 1610. He equated the *Fama* with the alchemical school of Paracelsus.[xiv] Clearly, whatever the date, there was an antecedence prior to 1614, as the book is the culmination of thought processes, and it certainly appears to have existed in some form or other prior to then. As to whether Christian Rosenkreutz ever existed or is an allegory, A. E. Waite would write:

> "The story of the *Fama Fraternitatis* is that of the mythical founder of the Rosy Cross ... a mythical personality implies a mythical foundation, in the sense that it is falsified historically."[xv]

Be he real or mythical, Christian Rosenkreutz's teachings were essentially esoteric alchemy, in which the Philosopher's Stone symbolized enlightenment. "The medieval Rosicrucian knew that all forms of love in the soul are what correspond to mercury" commented Rudolf Steiner.[xvi] This was because mercury is an incorruptible, fluid metal. Love was the Philosopher's Stone the *prima materia*. It was love that gave Socrates the strength not to abandon the people to save his own life; it was love that compelled Nestor to counsel Agamemnon; and it was love that inspired Aeneas to go through so many hardships to establish a new home for his people.

Olympus Possesses a Maro in Art

Olympus is a metaphor for Plato's Utopia. In this sense it does not matter to whom the verses refer. The point is that the attributes of genius work through love, the Philosopher's Stone.

The Latin epitaph is key to understanding the English verse below, as it is clear that personified Death is cheated by Virgil escorting Dante through Inferno. Virgil represents reason and wisdom, making him the perfect guide. As we have seen, Virgil's literary character of Aeneas made a journey to the underworld, and according to Roman mythology he was later deified. We are looking therefore at the Rosicrucian ideal of the golden ones. This is the secret of the monument.

There is no evidence that Shakespeare cared about immortalizing himself in stone, let alone having a grandiose final resting place. Just look at the facts: he likely never planned or paid for a monument; he was buried in the chancel of an obscure parish church (a position of prominence, true, but under a very simple stone); and his body appears to have been interred in a sackcloth (which people commonly chose in support of the English linen trade). Not exactly the actions of a narcissistic businessman, but rather an act of simple humility.

The socio-scientific agenda of the Rosicrucian movement was all that mattered, and this was Shakespeare's last act of genius: to request his friends erect a metaphor to honour the fraternity's values.

Chapter Three:
Stay, Passenger

Turning to the verses in English, one intuitively feels the poem was composed by Leonard Digges.

On the face of it, the poem calls on the passer-by (the "Passenger") to reflect on Shakespeare's brilliance as a writer, but of course there is much more to it than that. The reader is being petitioned to reflect on "Envious Death" and mortality, in much the same way as Digges' prologue laments that time will eventually dissolve the Stratford Monument. For me this is a clear indication that Digges, at least, was one of the subscribers. This theory finds support in the Church Monuments Society survey, which states:

> "Remarkable by its absence is any of the genealogy and biography in which Elizabethans and Jacobeans delighted. All we have by way of personal detail is Shakespeare's date of death and his age which are inserted at the bottom in smaller lettering. The rest is an epitaph, in two lines of Latin and six of English, of the type which several

poets contributed to the First Folio of his works, published in 1623. One of the poets in question was Jonson and the epitaph has been attributed to him. It rehearses a familiar theme of the period, derived from Horace, that a person's life and work are his true monument; the theme recurs, in much more lucid form, in his First Folio epitaph. The whole text shows every sign of having been added after the monument was erected. This strongly suggests that Shakespeare set up the monument to himself, following a common and well accepted practice of the time, leaving others to glorify him in verse and to specify when he died. If so, the effigy acquires a new interest and significance. In the twentieth century it did not get a good press. The famous Shakespearian scholar John Dover Wilson said it made the Bard look like a 'self-satisfied pork butcher'. It has been repainted more than once and if the later paint layers were removed some detail might be revealed which would improve the likeness."[xvii]

The poem shares Shakespeare's obsession with death and mortality. It is known that Shakespeare was acquainted with the works of his French contemporary, Michel de Montaigne (1533-1592), who famously wrote:

"Let us have nothing so much in minde as death. At the stumbling of a horse, at the fall of a stone, at the least prick with a pinne, let us presently ruminate and say with our selves, what if it were death it selfe?" Montaigne, *Essays*

A constant mindfulness of Envious Death is almost far eastern in its undertones, a theme that is not as strange as it seems when we consider the Rosicrucian influences on Shakespeare. The "Quick Nature" of which the poem speaks is the vitalism of the poet, life now departed, but whose works are far more valuable than the modest cost of the monument. The "Living Art" alludes to the effect on the audience and readers of all the Poet has written, rather than the dry physical page. That Digges is the author of these lines is likely, and most likely wrote them around the time of the First Folio when the monument was still fresh in his mind:

"When Brasse and Marble fade, shall make thee looke
Where, in eternal Brass remains thy Name.
Fresh to all Ages : when Posteritie
Unto thy voice Eternity hath given
Shall loath what's new, thinke all is prodegie
That is not Shake-speares; ev'ry Line, each Verse
Here shall revive, redeeme thee from thy Herse.
Nor Fire, nor cankring Age, as Naso said,
Of his, thy wit-fraught Booke shall once invade.
Nor shall I e're beleeve, or thinke thee dead."

Passengers are, by definition, in an act of movement, and the inference here is that the passer-by is sharing Shakespeare's journey towards the undiscovered country.

The page in the poem is sometimes equated with a servant, or someone of lesser status rather an actual page of paper. Either way, there are many reasons why the Living Art is greater than the manuscript. As inferred to already, it is the effect on the individual's feelings that matter. No one in literature has raised the nobility of humanity quite like Shakespeare. It is suggestive perhaps of the advantages of free-thought, by which means alone we may contemplate our limited time on earth. However, the expression "but page" is most likely referring to the fact that no one considered themselves worthy or good enough to follow in Shakespeare's footsteps. Nobody could fill the blank page with verse in imitation of him.

The poem is also an invitation to gain knowledge of the wit (wisdom) of the Master by reading his unsurpassable works and by watching the Living Art of its performance. There is little to add to this, save now to turn our attention to the masonic influences in the monument, before we turn our attention to Rosicrucianism.

Chapter Four:
Freemasonry?

Geometry is the mathematical system of visualising the numerical principles of the physical universe. In sacred geometry (indeed, wherever we consider the characteristics of dimension and numbers generally), we must also look to a mystical meaning. This may appear odd to those who do not ordinarily look for sacred geometry in the physical world of our ordinary senses. To the Elizabethans, however, this Divine code was perceivable everywhere about them. The Anglican Divine Richard Hooker (1554 –1600) summed up the world-view of the period in his classic book *Of the Lawes of Eccelesiastical Politie*:

> "The wise and learned amongst the very heathens themselves have all acknowledged some first cause whereupon originally the being of all things dependeth; neither have they otherwise spoken of that cause than as an agent, which knowing what and why it worketh, observeth in working a most exact order or law."

Hooker recognised a hierarchy from the First Cause and descending angels that influenced the earth:

> "Angels are spirits immaterial and intellectual, the glorious inhabitants of those sacred palaces where there is nothing but light and immortality; no shadow of matter for tears, discontentments, griefs, and uncomfortable passions to work upon;

but all joy, tranquillity, and peace, even forever and ever, do dwell."

The concealment of spirit in ordinary matter underlines a much deeper mystery still, namely that the material, elemental world is destined to pass from time, and to become one with the Divine world we cannot yet see. Until then it must be subjected to the present order. It was Jacob who saw a ladder or portal into the heavens, bearing the names of the seventy-two aeons of angels ascending and descending. Shakespeare and his contemporaries would have taken for granted the existence of an angelic hierarchy surrounding the throne of God. This was a common belief since ancient times and derived from the concept of God being the First Cause of everything that exists. This was expressed in the derivations of the Divine Name, and the names and the derivative numbers (powers) ascribed to the hierarchy of angelic beings, or aeons. These names were understood to contain all of the mysteries and all wisdom and were manifested from the seventy-two names of God mentioned in three verses on Exodus 14:19-21. The letters of these verses can be arranged into seventy-two triads of letters, and if the middle set are reversed in order, the seventy-two sequences become the seventy-two names of God. It was this tradition which influenced the apocalyptic literature found in the Revelation of St. John the Divine. We see these numbers in the geometric shapes above.

Science was in its infancy, and alchemy was regarded as a pseudo-scientific discipline at the time. Another means of controlling the environment was considered to be through the theurgical tradition of invoking the assistance of angelic entities through the invocation of their names. As a result, humanity had to make itself favourable to these spirit mediators, because the Divinity was too pure to be able to communicate directly with impure beings. Mastery of these techniques was held to have the following effects: (1) the acquisition of knowledge of the universe, of the primitive state of the immensity of space, time and all its forms; (2) acquisition of knowledge of the emanated spirits, both good and evil; (3) knowledge of the original state of man; and (4) knowledge of God.

The hope, the attempt, and the supposed result, of the theurgy practised by the sixteenth century magi such as John Dee and Paracelsus (c.1493-1541) was to obtain the assistance of entities operating under the seventy-two names of God. Paracelsus was highly influential, and wrote about the Four Ancients, the elemental supernatural beings existing below the order of angels and who corresponded to the classical elements and who played a part in the creation of the material universe: these Paracelsus named Salamanders (fire); Gnomes (earth); Undines (water); and Sylphs (air). In the process of transforming crude, physical matter as a means of reintegration with the Divinity, the alchemists became magi by reason of invoking supernatural mediators, the Beings of Living Light, indeed, even those elementals trapped in physical matter.

The two putti on the monument shown above represent Adam's labour with the trowel, and death by the inverted torch and skull. Entered Apprentice Freemasons will be familiar with the words used at the Charge to the initiate, where he is told that even kings have desired to "exchange the scepter for the trowel". Indeed, masonic candidates enter the Lodge for the first time "poor and penniless" and, just like the Passenger passing by Shakespeare's funerary monument, are commanded to reflect in humility on the superior learnings of the Master entombed within the temple.

The themes of labour and death or rest are by happenchance, Masonic. However, the trowel is interesting because it is not one of the speculative Working Tools. Originally, each initiate was given a trowel together with an apron, the significance of the former being of course the cementing process of building work. Nevertheless, the trowel was also a weapon, symbolising both the Spear of Destiny that pierced the side of Christ, and which also had a practical, operative function for a stonemason's self-defence. It should not surprise us therefore that at one time the Inner Guard in Freemasonry was armed with a sharp, pointed trowel. As for the inverted lamp, this may represent death or labour's rest at night, but it can just as easily be interpreted as light being dimmed for initiatory purposes, as occurs for the blindfolded initiate in the first degree, and in the darkened lodge of his raising in the third degree.

Shakespeare's coat of arms

Shakespeare's father was a gentleman with a coat of arms, and his son invested considerable time and money obtaining these for himself. It is unclear why Shakespeare wanted to do this, particularly after the death of Hamnet, but the reason appears to lie in the chivalric Quest for the so-called Philosopher's Stone or Holy Grail of alchemy. This is because a coat of arms is the symbol and motto of the Seeker, representing his intention on the Quest, and the way he passes from ignorance to self-realization. A coat of arms is a reminder as to how to go about life, and what direction the knightly-seeker should follow. The ego-mind easily gets led astray and sidetracked, therefore the coat of arms functions as a spiritual compass on that journey. It is clear that Shakespeare saw the acquisition of his coat of arms as a symbol of the chivalric quest, and the evidence lies in the symbolism contained in the arms he chose. The image of Shakespeare's coat of arms above is a reconstruction based on the words of the official grant. Although his coat of arms appear on the monument, we must rely on the grant for a description, because they were painted over in the eighteenth-century restoration:

> "Gold, on a bend, sable [black], a spear of the first, steeled argent [silver tip]; and for his crest... a falcon his wings displayed argent [silver], standing on a wreath of his colours supporting a spear gold, steeled as aforesaid, [i.e. silver] set upon a helmet with mantles and tassles,"

The heraldic motto *Non-Sans Droict* translates as "Not Without Right." Aside from the obvious connotation of the spears (that on the shield and that held by the falcon) referencing the family name, Shake-speare, it is interesting that a spear is incorporated as it conveys a double meaning – possibly the pointed masonic trowel. The use of the colour gold on Shakespeare's coat of arms recalls the golden ones of Plato's *Republic*, and the Rosicrucian brotherhood inspired by it. Gold also reminds us of the ovens by which the alchemists strove to perfect the elemental world through the assaying of gold by fire. Silver is also the alchemical colour for mercury.

The word alchemy derives from the Egyptian name for the country's fertile black soil, *al-kimiya*, which is another prominent colour in Shakespeare's arms (*"gold, on a bend, sable black"*). The sword, trowel or spear have early masonic significance, as noted above, since either a trowel or spear were originally a symbolic weapon for defence for the Inner Guard. In 1737 Chevalier Ramsey noted: "after the example set by the Israelites when they erected the Second Temple, who, whilst they handled the trowel and mortar with one hand, in the other held a sword and buckler."[xviii]

The spear in Catholicism also represents the Holy Lance (the Spear of Destiny or Longinus), whereby the blood and water of Christ were released from the *post mortem* stabbing of Christ's heart. This is one of the mysteries of the Catholic Church, and points to the dual nature of the God-Man incarnating on earth. It also carries alchemical symbolism too, since the red blood and white water are symbols of fire or vitality and spiritual water. The fiery-water of spirit is the *divina materia*. A significant "cost" indeed for Shakespeare to secretly import both a Catholic mystery and Rosicrucian icon into plain view in his public coat of arms.

The Spear of Destiny

The theme of duality is mirrored throughout the monument. The upside-down torch in the hand of the putto reminds us that each of these figures symbolise life and death, the extinguishment of the former being shown in the skull, the final symbol of the entire edifice, Envious Death:

The sandstone skull reminds us that the "Grand Lodge Above" is never far away. The vitality of life, the "Quick Nature" of the etheric force is soon removed from the physical body, and at which point the carnal form rapidly dissolves down into its constituent elements and parts as it decomposes. What remains after departing the physical body, depending on your point of view, are either the subtle spiritual bodies of a human being, or merely a record and memory of who we once were. The appeal on the monument for the passer-by to stop and reflect on mortality - what Montaigne described as the constancy of death - is a reminder of what befalls us all, at least in this physical life. Death can come at any time, as Shakespeare wrote:

> "Not a whit we defy augury; there's a special providence in the fall of a sparrow. If it be now, 'tis not to come, if it be not to come, it will be now' if it be not now, yet it will come. The readiness is all. Since no man has aught of what he leaves, what is't to leave betimes. Let it be."
> *Hamlet*, Act 5 verse 2

On one level, Shakespeare's immortality resides in his writings, and the monument begs us to take heed of these. There is a hint of the here-after in the poem, since Living Art conquers Envious Death.

The skull is a profoundly masonic symbol, too. In Masonic Templarism it represents mortality. The appearance of a skull and bones in the third degree ceremony of raising in Craft Masonry carries the same meaning, and also alludes to Hiram Abif and the three ruffians as allegories of Abel, Cain and his evil sisters. Thus, the skull represents the ancient fall of man into further degradation and decay. In other words, it is a stark reminder of what we are, and how far we have fallen from that we once were.

The polished black marble Corinthian columns are typical supports found in many Elizabeth and Jacobean monuments of the period. They obviously have an architectural purpose in supporting the entablature and provide visual asymmetry. However, as with everything in this construction, they also carry a number of alternative meanings.

Jachin and Boaz, print circa 1650

In the first Temple at Jerusalem there were two free-standing columns placed in front of the Sanctuary containing the Holy of Holies, where the Shekinah or Spirit of God dwelt on earth. In the masonic tradition, the Temple pillars were made by Hiram Abif at the request of king Solomon. The Bible itself merely records that Hiram, king of Tyre, sent materials and builders to Jerusalem (2 Samuel 5:11 and 1 Kings 5:1-10). 1 Kings 7:15 states the pillars were made of nehoshet, a pure copper or bronze. Superficially they represented God's strength and his eternal covenant with the chosen people. They also allegorised the pillars of cloud by day and fire by night that accompanied the Hebrews during their flight from Egypt.[xix] The trowel and inverted lamp held by the cherubim on Shakespeare's monument

58

suggest an intended connection with the Temple pillars, as the pillars conveyed several other dual themes.

Each column was divided into two parts: the stem was eighteen cubits (thirty feet) high, and the capital was five cubits. The total height of each was therefore twenty-three cubits. The description of Solomon's Temple given in Josephus[xx] tells us that the entrance was between these two, equal columns. The one on the right was called Jachin which means "to establish", and the one on the left was called Boaz meaning "in strength."

> "He [Solomon] set up the pillars in front of the temple, one on the south, the other on the north; that on the south he called Jachin, and that on the north Boaz." 2 Chronicles 3:17

However, there is another occult tradition that the true import of the name Boaz is "confusion" (although perhaps it is more accurately intended to be "chaos"). Esoterically, the pillars allude to the incorporation of Adam into his dual male and female correspondences. They therefore represent opposition, sex-energy and self-generation. Both were equal because the spiritual being of man and woman share the same origins, the same emanation from God and have the same work to fulfil.

Jachin announces the power of creative command that God gave Adam and represents the Tree of Life; whereas Boaz expresses that which resulted from Adam's prevarication: a repetition of the fall of the angels (symbolized by the Tree of Knowledge of Good and Evil). The Temple pillars therefore represent the two opposing branches of Severity and Mercy in the Kabbalistic Tree of Life, itself an allegory of that which grew in the Garden of Eden (opposite the Tree of Knowledge of Good and Evil (that is, of hubris and pride). Yet, in truth, there is only one pillar, albeit there *appear* to be two:

> "And the angel of God, which went before the camp of Israel, removed and went behind them; and the pillar of the cloud went from before their face, and stood behind them: and it came between the camp of the Egyptians and the camp of Israel; and it was a cloud and darkness to them, but it gave light by night to these: so that the one came not near the other all the night." Exodus 14:19-20

Humanity, despite Adam's fall, has always had the same work to fulfil and for which it was destined by God. It must work for its reconciliation. In the Secret Tradition this is the only means of re-establishing balance to our true quaternary nature (that is, our physical body, etheric form, mind and spirit), so as to take back from the fallen angels the authority reserved to us. In esoteric Freemasonry, the geographic direction of the south symbolises the mind of man; the north is man's vitality; the west his body; and In the east his spirit (that which connects him with God). Thus, the opposites of the south and north highlight that man is weakest in the mind where the godless spirits are relegated; whereas his vitalism (that which gives life to the body, the temple of the spirit) must be inhabited by the good spirits responsible for containing them. In the Bible, Cain is banished to the south with his sisters. It is therefore no coincidence that the Shakespeare monument is erected at the north-east of the church, because this mirrors the position of the Holy of Holies in the Jerusalem Temple and implies the invocation of significant spiritual forces in the strengthening of man's vitality (his "quick nature") and spirit. Indeed, this is the reason why the masonic initiate stands in the North East corner of the lodge at his initiation.

Elizabethan and Jacobean cosmology was such that the immutable decrees of God must always have their fulfilment. The person who delivered a contrary will to God's plan contradicted the designs of the Creator and renounced his original destination as a spiritual being. The name Jachin announces the power of command over the fallen angels which is reserved for man in principle; but Boaz expresses that which results following sin.

The columns also symbolise the two mythical pillars known as the Lost Pillars of Enoch, which contained all knowledge of science, and which were submerged by the Deluge (Noah's Flood). One was said to have been made of stone, the other of mud brick. The first, that of stone, was raised in the direction of the North by the descendants of Seth, Adam's third son; the other column had been raised in the south by the descendants of Cain. Again we have the confluence here of the direction of north and south with that of good and evil, or truth and error, etc. The former foresaw the strength and stability of good spiritual works, and resisted the floods in the Deluge, and was preserved for a long time afterwards; the other announced the weakness and corruption of the works of matter, which was even designated by the number of confusion in its proportions. So, it was totally destroyed by the waters of the Deluge, along with Cain's posterity.

Josephus wrote that the surviving stone pillar could still be seen in Syria. It was said to be from this column that the ancient scribes of Mesopotamia and Egypt rediscovered writing and the secrets of alchemy. Hermes Trismegistos ("Hermes the Thrice-Great") is the mythological amalgamation of the Greek god Hermes (the "Messenger") and the Egyptian god Thoth (the deity of, among other things, wisdom and learning). Hermes Trismegistos imparted knowledge of the secrets he found on the tablets in Egyptian temples, and was the purported author of the *Hermetica,* which formed the basis of a number of philosophical, alchemical and theurgical systems known as Hermeticism. It is said of the mythical Christian Rosenkreutz that he journeyed to the Middle East and Egypt to learn these secrets and brought Seth's ancient knowledge back to medieval Western Europe.

Whilst presented as opposites, the pillars also have a unity of type and represent the divine, fiery substance of the one, living God. We simply do not know if Shakespeare's monument memorialises the Temple pillars in all their diverse and colourful array of symbolic beauty, but we do have to take into account the following clues:

- the putti represent life and death; labour and rest;
- the contrasting opposites in the anonymous poem, i.e. Envious Death who cannot overshadow Shakespeare's immortality;
- the contrast of mortality and immortality in the Latin verse.

It is likely that the columns fuse the messages contained in the two inscriptions, and as such are less a memorial or epitaph to Shakespeare than a message "from beyond the grave." This is nothing less than a petition to acquire the self-knowledge of our true, spiritual natures as the descendants of Adam's son, Seth. If we consider the page and quill held by the figure of Shakespeare, we can also see an allusion to the Lost Pillars of Enoch: the quill in the hand of the Master whose "Living Art" preserves his wisdom; the other a blank page washed clear by death.

Chapter Five:
The Kabballah

The Passenger might not take much notice of the monument's three supporting carved stone corbels. They obviously serve a primary architectural purpose of fixing the structure to the wall, presumably with metal dowels and cramps. However, an interesting symmetry

is made by them, and which remind us of the deeply
Kabbalistic clues contained within the memorial:

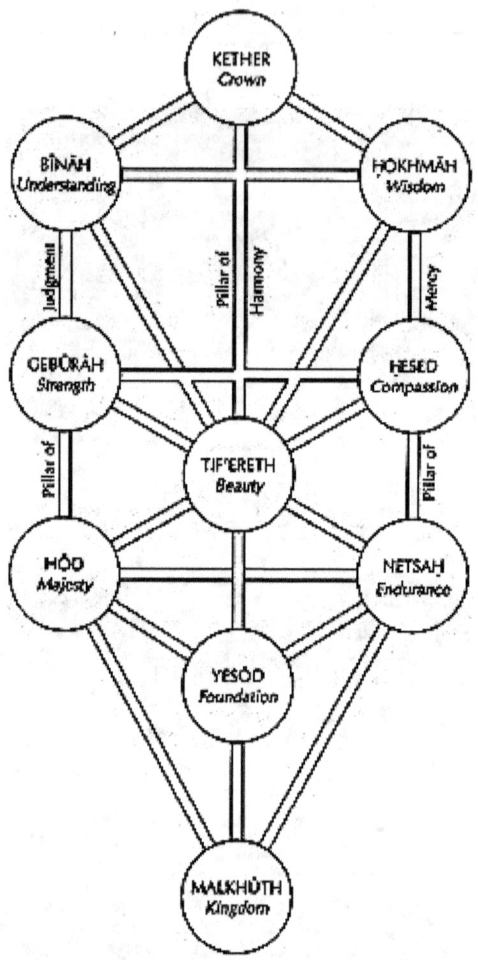

Etz Hayim, the Kabbalistic Tree of Life

Indeed, the overall impression of the structure lends
itself to a Kabbalistic interpretation, or a version thereof.

The two inscriptions above the stone corbels might
allude to the lower sephira of Yesod and Malkuth, or
Foundation (the ordinary world). The left-hand column
under the putto of labour that of Hod (majesty), and that

64

on the right Nezach, endurance. Shakespeare himself appears to represent the sephirot Tiferet, meaning Beauty or Truth. The Corinthian cornices correspond with Geburah and Chesed, or Judgement and Mercy. Directly beneath the putto on the left is Binah, Understanding, and that on the right is Chesed, Wisdom. Shakespeare himself is therefore the gate or portal in the centre of the three columns leading straight to Kether, the Crown, representing bliss. This is occupied by the skull, serving to remind us that the Middle-Path is a direct access to Kether, found in the wisdom of his works and which can be learned in this life. I have to agree with Dawkins that the arched niche occupied by the demi-figure is indeed a stylised gateway,[xxi] as the monument itself clearly implies this.

What is intended is the Middle-Path of the Kabbalah, where wisdom and the working tools of the subject are the means by which we may attain entrance to Kether. There is however a state beyond even Kether, which the Kabbalists call Ein Sof (meaning "infinite"). Ein Sof is God in his unmanifested state, outside of both time and space.

It will also be noted that in the *Zohar* (*The Book of Wisdom*) the mountains Abraham and Moses ascend are allegories of portals or entranceways to Divinity. They were regarded as having an "eighth" portal or door. This is also mirrored in the disappearance of the Old Testament prophet Enoch,[xxii] who lived a symbolical three hundred and sixty five years before he was "taken" by God when he "was no more." This was not a punishment for Enoch, but a reward for the completion of his visible works. Indeed, Enoch is an ar*chetype of* Man Restored. 1 Enoch chapter 81:1-3 states:

> "Now, my son Mathusala, all these things I speak unto thee, and write for thee. To thee I have revealed all and have given thee books of

everything. Preserve, my son Mathusala, the books written by thy father; that thou mayest transmit them to future generations.

"Wisdom have I given to thee, to thy children, and thy posterity, that they may transmit to their children, for generations for ever, this wisdom in their thoughts; and that those who comprehend it may not slumber, but hear with their ears; that they may learn this wisdom, and be deemed worthy of eating this wholesome food."

The raised position of the structure over the window symbolizes how earthly light is limited in relation to the ancient, unmanifest light of the Ein Sof, as with a torch compared to the light of the Sun. This is what the putti holding the inverted torch signifies.

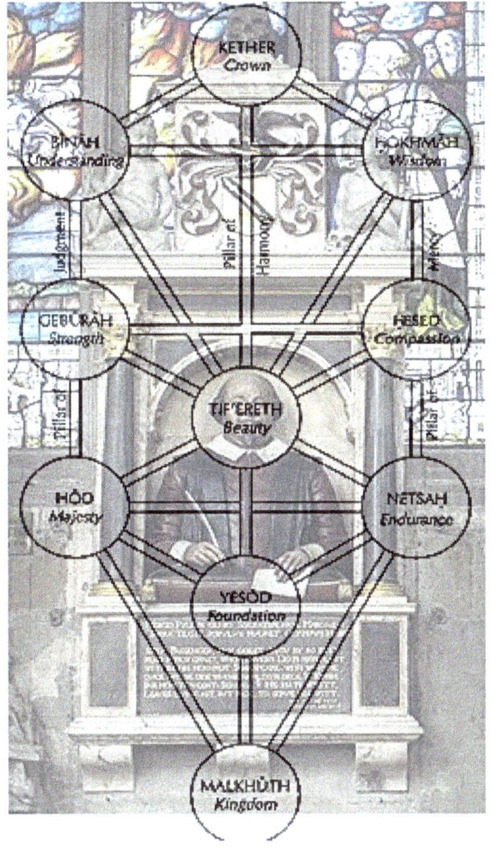

In Kabbalistic terms, the winding, serpentine paths through the realms or sephira on the Tree of Life[xxiii] (Etz Hayim) can be represented in both positive and negative ways. There are thirty-two paths. The inverse of thirty-two is twenty-three, and the twenty-third path of the Kabballah is called "the House of Consciousness", alluding to that between Hod and Geburah (which ties in with the Tarot twelve trump or Hanging Man card I mention later). On this path the initiate learns that his immortal personality, his soul, or mind, exists between two metaphorical pillars, or columns. These are the intellect and instinct, or man's spiritual and animal natures (otherwise the pillars of fire by night and cloud by day), by which God raised the consciousness of the people.

In the Kabballah, the two outlying columns are symbolized by the sephira Hod (intellect) and Netzach (instinct). Along the ascending path of reintegration - as opposed to the descending path of encampment in the four alchemical elements - the twenty-third path of the Kabballah takes the initiate to the sephirot Hod to acquire knowledge. This leads to a vision of the "Eternal Splendour" of the opposite pillar of Chessed, or mercy, a harmonisation which leads to Kether, the Kingdom of Heaven (which must first be seen, and from whence the Son of Man descended into lower elemental form). Hod is the terminus of the Pillar of Severity or Form, the receptacle of the "substance of the Unity", the fifth element of spirit, the prima materia. The opposite Pillar of Mercy is the receptacle of the "splendour of the Unity" and the Middle Pillar, the receptacle of "holy power". In Hod, the splendour is only perceived by the intellect, which was Nicodemus' problem in the Gospel of John. The reflection of this splendour was contained in the burnished bronze of the Brazen Serpent raised by Moses, and then by Solomon in the form of the Temple bronze pillars. The splendour cannot be experienced in its wholeness on earth, and hence why physical death is but the first stage of transformation.

We need to reconsider the columns to explain this. Universal duality is often symbolised in alchemy by the opposite colours black and white, and which is why there is a quill and a white sheet of paper shown in the monument. Much has been made of the blank page, but it is essentially a metaphor for duality appearing in the monument in its many guises: the columns; the putti; the 'living' figure of the poet and the 'dead' skull, and so forth. In this context, the cushion is most probably representing the pillow as a symbol of comfort. The Middle-Path is by definition the most direct and comforting of them all. The duality of the columns and the other dualisms we have noted, represent strength and weakness; sex-energy; Cain and Abel; good and bad; thought and action; creativity and inactivity etc. The list goes on and is only limited by the imagination. The columns, just like the twin pillars of Mercy and Severity in the Kabballah, symbolise the mystery of opposition that exists throughout creation, and which stand astride the 'pillar' of equilibrium of balance leading direct to Kether.

Now, much has been made of the dates of Shakespeare's birth and death. Also, the numerological significance of the dates as they appear on his monument. It cannot be coincidental that Shakespeare wrote *Hamlet*, his greatest play on the twin themes of death and grief after the death of his only son, Hamnet. Neither is it coincidental that Yorick has decayed in the earth some "three and twenty years." Dawkins makes much of the date of Shakespeare's death and the fact that it states his age as fifty-three not fifty-two. The obvious point is that everyone, Shakespeare himself, may have thought he was a year older. Putting that issue aside, the point made by Peter Dawkins in his paper for the Francis Bacon Research Trust is that the false age given for Shakespeare of fifty-three has geometrical significance, in this instance the 53° right-angled triangle.[xxiv] However, I believe this conclusion to be wrong, albeit that he is correct that there are Pythagorean and Hermetic principles at play in the number fifty-three (and which may be a clue that that the monument is essentially Kabbalistic).

Geometry is the mathematical system of visualising the numerical principles of the physical universe, and we see this in the carefully structured patterns contained in the monument. Pythagoras (570-495 BC) held that all things were made of numbers and, like the ancient Chinese of whom he had no knowledge, believed numbers were either masculine or feminine in character. They therefore contained the sex energy or force of the opposing principles of generation found in nature.

For instance, even numbers were held to contain feminine passive energy, and odd numbers active, masculine energy. In his system, the number five therefore represented marriage and harmony, because it was the sum of the number two (the feminine principle) and the number three (the masculine principle), applying the formula: $2 + 3 = 5$. To reinforce this, the Pythagoreans taught that $2 \times 5 = 10$, and $1 + 0 = 1$, which they regarded as the "perfect number". The number one symbolised unity and God. This was therefore a very different interpretation of the number five to that taken by the Rosicrucians.

If we look at the number twenty-three, there are observations worthy of note concerning it. The number eleven is regarded in certain esoteric Christian traditions as the number associated with death. This is because it equates with the number two ($11 = 1 + 1$, and $1 + 1 = 2$) and the double energy of individuality and imbalance. The negative connotation of the numbers two or twenty (the latter by designation of the formula $20 = 2 + 0 = 2$) represent opposition, incompatibility, and negative forces. The number three represents weakness and narcissism (and numerologically is derived by the formula of $1+1+1 = 3$ or $2 + 1 = 3$). The combination of two or twenty and three is equated with the number five in numerology (following the numerological formula of $2 + 3 = 5$, or $2 + 0 + 3 = 5$). Five is a number said to represent discord and suffering. However, twenty-three has the following peculiar characteristics:[xxv]

It must also be acknowledged that the number twenty-three has some curious characteristics: each parent contributes twenty-three chromosomes to a foetus (there are forty-six chromosomes in human bodies, made from twenty-three pairs); the average human biorhythm is twenty-three days; blood takes 23 seconds to circulate the body; the human spine is generally composed of thirty-two vertebrae; the natural number of permanent teeth is thirty-two; the earth's axis is tilted at twenty-three degrees; twenty-three is one of the most cited prime numbers in mathematics a prime number, can only be divided by itself and the number one (but which is true of all primes); and twenty-three is the lowest prime that consists of consecutive digits, the building block of all mathematics.

For the Pythagoreans, the number twenty-three was reducible to five by applying the decadic system (2+3=5). Tellingly, Pythagoras held that this was the number of movement, symbolizing duality coming into peace, love and harmony. This is the very point and purpose of the middle column of equilibrium in the Kabballah. Thus, if we consider the fundamental form of the square forming the central focus of the Stratford monument, we count five symbols: the poet, his pen, the page and the pillow.

Remember also that the Latin verses of the epitaph follow a formula of two and three as well. We have three columns comprised of two lines each:

When the two opposite forces merge, their energy is greater than the sum of their individual parts, leading to the attributes represented by the Poet. The number three is symbolized by the triangle, the perfect balancing of two opposite elements by a third mediating component. It therefore represents balance and harmony. This is also the true meaning of the number fifty-three on Shakespeare's monument. It is deliberately wrong (he was fifty-two) but is a code of numerological reduction where chaos (two) is brought into balance by the creative forces of opposition (three).

Fifty-three by numerological reduction obtains the number eight, by reason of 5+3=8. Eight represents harmony united with the creative outcome of the opposing dual forces, as just described. In Hebrew, the numerical value of the first letter in the alphabet aleph א is one, but pictographically it is formed of two yods (yod is the tenth letter of the alphabet) and the letter vau ו (the sixth letter). This gives aleph a numerological value of one and eight by reason of the numerological addition 2+6=8. Alpeh is also one letter made of three parts. In alchemical terms, the attributes are represented by metals (lead, silver and gold - which are the colours of Shakespeare's coat of arms) and also by the elements (salt, sulphur and mercury). Mercury is the fourth element that stabilises the imbalance between the three metallic substances and the three elemental forms since it is both a metal and an element, unchanging, incorruptible and formless. It has the characteristics of elemental water but the attributes of metal.

The number four is symbolized by the square, which represents the physical world imbued with spirit. In us, therefore, the sensible soul adds the number four to our triadic form of spirit, mind (soul) and body, and in the incarnation of Christ the number is doubled in his person, since Christ unified from his human mother the four-fold nature of humanity's soul, spirit, body and mind with his the divine sensible soul, spirit, body and mind, thus 4+4=8 in the person of Christ's incarnation on earth.

Fifty-three may therefore be said to be the number of the perfected man, the fully integrated human being who has attained Kether and union with God. Yet, Shakespeare was not fifty-three but fifty-two when he died, and the significance of this to any passing Rosicrucian is that such perfection and union is impossible in the temporal material world in which we exist. It can only be attained in the world to come. The message on the monument is therefore that while Shakespeare came as close as any living person to the attainment of eternal wisdom, his journey continues elsewhere. His family knew this, as did his friends. Hence, I submit, the message in the working tool of the page of paper is that no more can be written or learned by him in this life, but that he is prepared for the next. Yet, what if the page is symbolically reversed? What

might be conveyed then? What secrets might it contain?
I suspect that if this is what is implied by the page, then
the message must be that we have to find the answers
for ourselves.

The dual confluence of the numbers two, three and five
in combination in geometrical terms, as the six-sided
Seal or Ring of Solomon, often depicted in a pentagram
or geometric hexagon and other variant forms, unifying
the three-fold nature of man (body, soul and spirit)
interconnecting with the corresponding triune Divine
attributes of Thought, Will and Action. Numerically, the
number six is both the sum and product of its factors: 1
+ 2 + 3 = 6; and 1 x 2 x 3 = 6, and therefore represents
correspondence, symmetry, and balance.

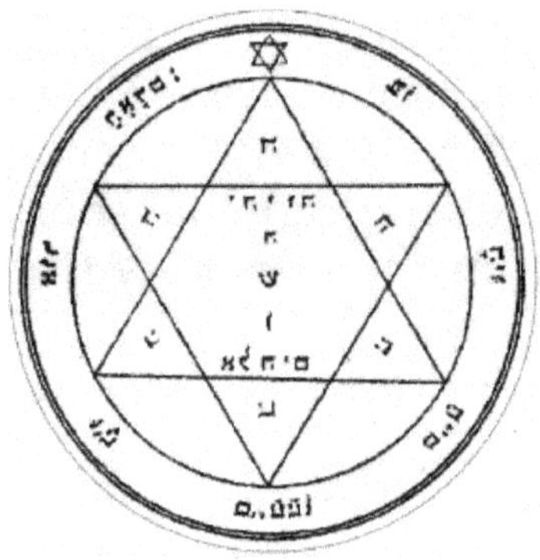

Opened outwards, the six-sided Seal of Solomon forms a dual triangle or a four-sided "perfect" square, representing the world and the classical elements. According to Paracelsus, the material substances are comprised of salt, sulphur and mercury (the *tria prima* or primal trinity). These give rise to the four elements of earth, air, fire and water. These can recombine into the *tria prima* by way of a combination of fire and air, air and water, and earth and water. This symbolises spirit or the mediating energy that carries the soul into the body - an integrating power combining both soul and spirit into physical form. On a quantum level, it is through these forces and essentials that all matter is generated. The skull tells us that death is but a process of the change of form, from one stage of alchemical transformation to another.

However, returning to the twenty-three (or two and three) Pythagorean theory of movement towards balance, the true *quaternary* nature of man (that is, his body, etheric form, astral body and ego or soul) is in passage towards union with the fifth element of spirit (the *prima materia* of the Divinity). This is symbolized by the pentagram as follows:

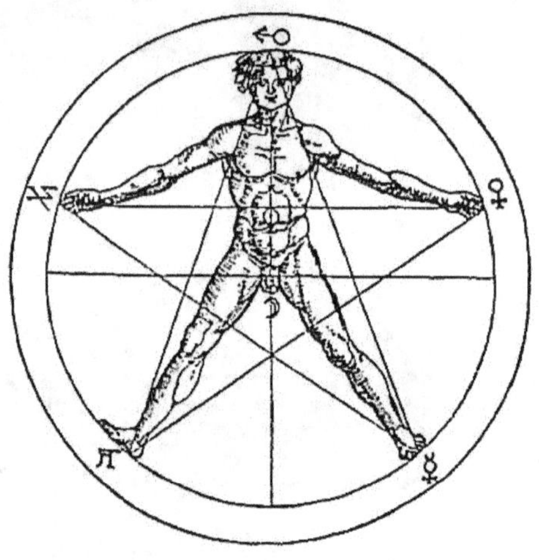

Factor in the four-fold or quaternary aspects of nature (the traditional alchemical elements of earth, wind, fire and water, symbolising the Divine-sensitive Spirit, minor spirit, mind and body present in man) then we end up with a ten-sided geometrical form which can only represent one thing: the Monad or Divine Unity itself:

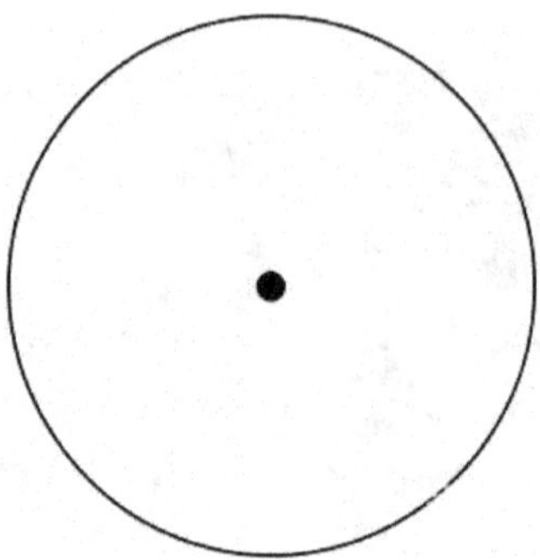

Geometrically, the ten-sided form is reducible to one, or the circle by process of reduction, 1+0+1=1. This then forms the eternal form or "0".

We might conclude that the Kabballah is best conceived or understood in the mind but realised by feeling. On duality this should be seen in terms of the generative forces of the masculine and feminine sex energy we find in number, which underpins creation. This ascent might be likened to a deeper, fully conscious awareness of the Four Worlds of the Kabballah: the Archetypical World, the Creative World, the Formative World and the Manifest or Material World. Right moral action, the formation of right mindfulness, the creation of a new self and spiritual intimacy with God are the objectives of the Kabbalist, and one cannot help but feel there is a connection between these ideals and the expressionless figure of Shakespeare holding his quill and blank page in the monument. This perennial movement between the Divine and the material on the middle path is reflected in the allegory of Jacob's Ladder as described in Genesis:

> "And he dreamed, and behold a ladder set up on the earth, and the top of it reached to heaven; and behold the angels of God ascending and descending on it." Genesis 28:12

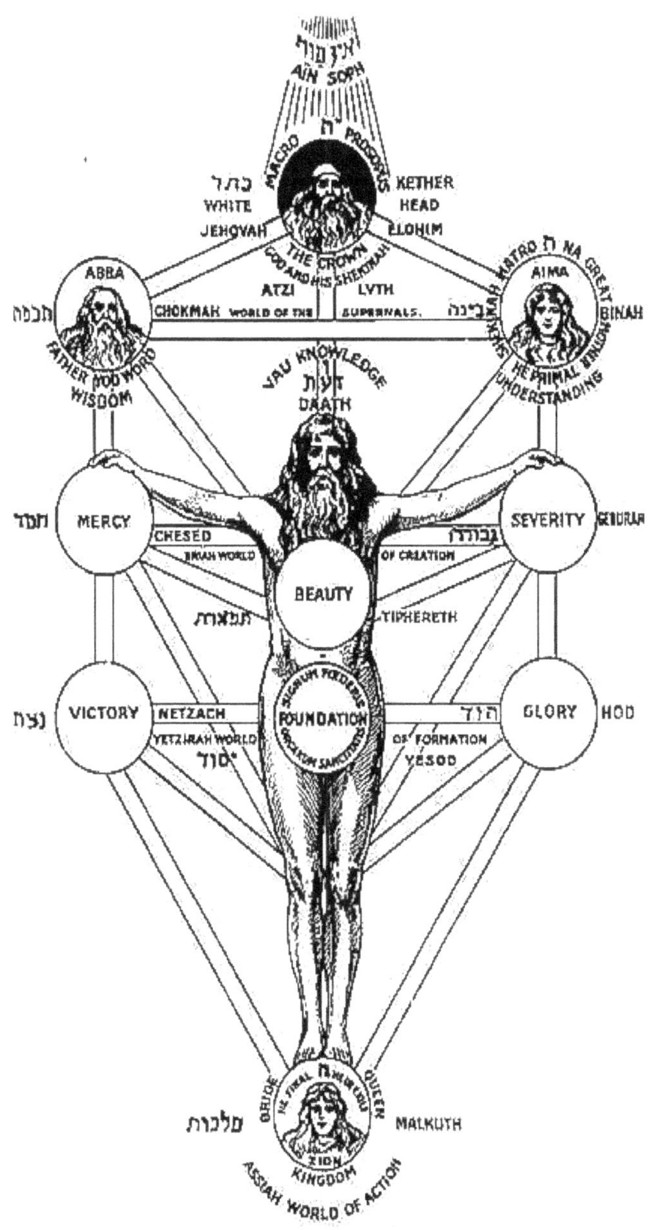

AIN SOPH
MACRO PROSOPUS
KETHER
WHITE
HEAD
JEHOVAH
ELOHIM
THE CROWN
GOD AND HIS SHEKINAH
ABBA
AIMA
MATRO NA GREAT MOTHER
CHOKMAH
ATZI LUTH
BINAH
WORLD OF THE SUPERNALS
FATHER GOD WORD
HE PRIMAL ENIGMA
WISDOM
UNDERSTANDING
VAU KNOWLEDGE
DAATH
MERCY
SEVERITY
GEBURAH
CHESED
BRIAH WORLD OF CREATION
BEAUTY
TIPHERETH
FOUNDATION
VICTORY
GLORY
HOD
NETZACH
YESOD
YETZIRAH WORLD OF FORMATION
QUEEN
BRIDE
HE FINAL
MALKUTH
ZION
KINGDOM
ASSIAH WORLD OF ACTION

Chapter Six: The Ciphers

Some have argued that the number thirty-three is a code embedded in the Latin epitaph, and indeed there may be some merit in this theory, even if we discount this a "Simple Cipher" for Francis Bacon.[xxvi]

"Wise and creative governance by the people in Utopia"

"The people desire the hidden genius of art"

If we remove the six larger letters, there are indeed sixty-six smaller letters in total. This clearly is a hidden cipher (I agree), but the numbers six, twelve (shown above), thirty-three, sixty-six and seventy-two all have deep esoteric significance on their own merit. Indeed, this is a more plausible position than the tortuous efforts of the Francis Bacon Research Trust to derive the name F. BACON from it. Consider the larger letters above: IPSMTO. Sure, the I is a J, but it is intentionally not carved that way. The letters are an anagram of the Latin word POSTIMO, which is the inflection of *postim*, meaning a doorpost or gateway. Interesting, right? Well, now consider the highlighted words as a sentence in their own right: *Iudicio Pylium Socrates Maronem Terra Olympus.* A simple translation of the intended meaning might be: "The judgement of Nestor, Socrates and Virgil in the land of Olympus"; but a likely meaning might be: "Wise and creative governance by the people in Utopia."

This leaves us with the remaining words in the sentence: *Genio Arte Tegit Populus Maeret Habet*: "the genius of art is buried and the people grieve"; or perhaps its true meaning might be: "The people desire the hidden genius of art." The two sentences are clearly contrasting Utopia and ideal governance with a sense of loss and repression. The entire seventy-two letter verse says essentially the same thing. Interestingly and as an aside, the number seventy-two has twelve divisions, and a factorisation value of 2 x 2 x 2 x 3 x 3.

You will hopefully by now appreciate how the first ten numbers, or decad, are numerologically reducible to the first nine. Fractal mathematics also determines patterns containing smaller and smaller versions of numbers. For example, in Dante Alighieri's *Divina Comedia,* there are repeated fractal structures which emphasise his cosmogony. Each of Dante's poems employs a decad structure, which is devised on a 9+1=10 basis for each of hell, purgatory and heaven, since the nine circles each have an additional portal or gateway that does not fully conform to the other nine layers. Thus, in Dante's *Inferno,* beyond the gateway or vestibule to hell is Limbo. The frightening inscription *Lasciate ogne speranza, voi ch'intrate* ("Abandon all hope, ye who enter here") greets the 'passengers' passing through it. This in turn leads to the nine circles, where sinners are punished. There are therefore nominally nine circles, but in truth Dante's hell is divided into twenty-four spheres of nine circles plus a gateway in each (hence a decad). The number three is therefore the fractal pattern in Dante's cosmogony and represents the Divine Unity.

The letters do not signify Bacon, but God, because there are seventy-two, and the fractal number in the engraving is three:

- There are 66 uncapitalised letters
  6+6=12 and 1+2=3
- There are 12 words 1+2=3
- 66 + 6 = 72
- 7+2=9 (3x3)

It is nonsense that the double letters "TT" stand for the masonic thirty-third degree. Craft Masonry only has three degrees, albeit there are thirty-three degrees in the Rose Croix Chapter. The cipher in Craft Freemasonry is not TT but the Hebrew letter gimmel ג which is presented as a Latinised "G" in open lodge. Its gematric significance is the number three.

To be clear, I am not disputing that TT may refer to thirty-three, merely that it has no relevance as a cipher for Bacon, or the thirty-third degree in Rose Croix Freemasonry. The golden rule with all esoteric knowledge of a good and benevolent disposition is that it is available to everyone; and it is only a question of how to look. Thus, if we consider that there are four Ts carefully aligned in the English verse (which is obviously the case), the significance can only be that some form of gematria is intended. What we first notice is the visual form of a cross from the Ts, thus:

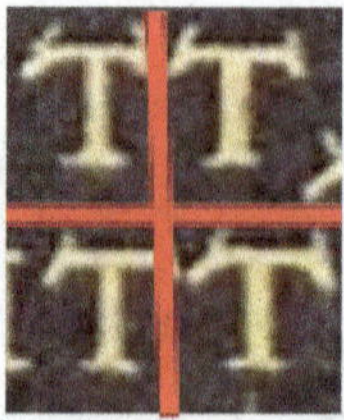

This may represent the four corners of the earth, or the classical elements of which this world was said to be made. They read downwards and diagonally, as well as across. There are twelve permutations:

 Thus, it may be another reference to the triadic symbolism apparent throughout the monument, since 1+2=3.

 Another theory is that T is the latinized Hebrew letter tau (the twenty-second and final letter of that alphabet), or else the Greek tau (the nineteenth letter of that alphabet). No doubt, like his contemporaries Shakespeare believed in the mystic powers of number. In Hebrew gematria the tau corresponds to the number four hundred, or four by reduction and which, in turn, alludes in alchemical lore to the four classical elements of which all life is composed. Gematria is essential to Hebrew Kabballah, which adheres to a cosmological system based on the creation of the universe by God, through the acoustic sound of certain Hebrew letters and their numerical values. In Greek gematria the tau has a numerical value of three hundred, which fits more comfortably with the repetition of the number three throughout the monument. Indeed, the Greeks used the tau as a symbol for measurement, as it is a mathematical constant representing a complete one-turn i.e. the length of any circle's circumference divided by the length of its radius, or two-times Pi (π) radius which is 360∘ Why four tau? It is either an allusion to the mystical value of the number nine (1440=9) the number of man in material form, or else it is an allusion to Pythagorean geometry since there are four tau (eight-times π radius) which divided by eight which becomes 22.5∘ representing the north-east degree or 1/16th of a circle.

The tau was considered a symbol of healing by the Crusaders because they believed Moses' bronze serpent had been affixed to a staff in the shape of a cross. This helps explain the form of the raised bronze serpent as depicted in certain high grade Freemasonic orders today, which may owe their origins to the initiatory rites and symbolism of the medieval craft guilds infiltrated by returning Crusader artisans. The tau also served as the blood-mark in the account of the Angel of Death during the tenth plague of Egypt:

> "And the blood shall be to you for a token upon the houses where ye are: and when I see the blood, I will pass over you, and the plague shall not be upon you to destroy you, when I smite the land of Egypt." Exodus 12:13

The tau may therefore have been understood as a collective mark of pardon or mercy, and as a reminder of the immanence of God in nature. Indeed, it is interesting that in ancient times the tau was used as a symbol for life or death. The association of a serpent on a tau cross has long been established with the medical profession. Here it appears on the cover of one of the first books of medicine, printed in 1546, the *Hippocratis Coi Medicorum Omnium:*

The Twelfth Trump Card, The Hanged Man

The tau cross also appears in the Tarot. Whilst Tarot cards are still commonly used for conventional card games, in the English-speaking world they are reserved almost exclusively for occult use and divination. The Hanged Man is the twelfth card in the Major Arcana of the Tarot deck and depicts an image of a man being hanged upside-down from his left foot. The tree from which he hangs is in the shape of a tau. A. E. Waite suggested that the image represents "life in suspension."

In Waite's words:

"I will say very simply on my own part that it expresses the relation, in one of its aspects, between the Divine and the Universe. He who can understand that the story of his higher nature is imbedded in this symbolism will receive intimations concerning a great awakening that is possible and will know that after the sacred Mystery of Death there is a glorious Mystery of Resurrection."[xxvii]

These are significant claims but are suggestive of the Real Presence of God in nature. Although the suspended man is in a position where he is unable to control his situation, at the same time he is conscious of it. Indeed, the hanged man purposefully crosses his right leg, to form either a fylfot cross or the Hebrew letter lamed (ל). The significance of the heraldic fylfot is geometric since it is a cross with four perpendicular extensions at 90° angles. The lamed is the twelfth letter in the Hebrew alphabet, and its appearance in the twelfth Major Arcana in the Tarot cannot be coincidental. It must surely reflect the Biblical use of the tau as a token to distinguish the repentant from the unrepentant.

The tau as a mark was also used to protect the reprobate Cain after murdering the righteous Abel:

"And the Lord said unto him: 'Therefore whosoever slayeth Cain, vengeance shall be taken on him sevenfold.' And the Lord set a mark upon Cain, lest any finding him should kill him. And the Lord said unto him, 'Therefore whosoever slayeth Cain, vengeance shall be taken on him sevenfold.'"
Genesis 4:15

In the book of Revelation, the tau again features as a seal or mark, this time to be placed on those who are to be spared the suffering of the Armageddon:

"And I saw another angel ascending from the east, having the seal of the living God: and he cried with a loud voice to the four angels, to whom it was given to hurt the earth and the sea, saying, 'Hurt not the earth, neither the sea, nor the trees, till we have sealed the servants.'" Revelation 7:2-3

More curious still, is the account in *The Trial of the Vowels* by the ancient Greek satirist Lucian of Samosata (AD 125 – 180), who composed a comedic "trial" of the vowel letters by the consonants. In the trial, the Greek letter Sigma accuses the Hebrew tau of inventing the model for crucifixion, i.e. suffering, and demands it be executed in its own shape:

> "Men weep, and bewail their lot, and curse Cadmus with many curses for introducing Tau into the family of letters; they say it was his body that tyrants took for a model, his shape that they imitated, when they set up the erections on which men are crucified."[xxviii]

The above symbol is used by the Egyptian Coptic Church. It incorporates the *crux ansata* (the ancient ankh, a symbol of eternal life) with the Christian cross. It is also the tau captained by a circle, representing God, and infinity. It is at once a symbol of life, divinity, resurrection, and resistance (the Copts resisted the Islamic invaders and were then branded with this mark to set them apart from their Arab neighbours).

Finally, the thirty-second path of the Kabballah is termed the "Path of the Tau", and represents a much lower evolutionary progression, that from the animal to the spiritual form. The link is that of the lowest sephirot Malkuth, representing the earth, to Yesod, which is located close to Malkuth and permits movement from one condition to another. It is therefore a two-stage movement from elemental form towards the formation of a higher consciousness, which is the promise of what may follow from such progress. The Kabbalistic Tree of Life then branches into the three separate paths or branches of severity, mercy and the middle way or pillar of spiritual enlightenment. There is therefore a significant difference between the inverse twenty-third and thirty-second paths, both of which reflect the interplay of order and chaos within the Divine Code. The four T's or tau letters therefore equate to the thirty-second path being multiplied by the power of four: 32+32+32+32=128, or 2 by reduction (1+2+8=11 and 1+1=2). It therefore equates to a sign warning about the dual conflicting forces of mercy and judgement, order and chaos.

Chapter Seven:
Kether, the Crown

In what respect might the skull symbolize Kether? On the surface it is a curious metaphor for eternal felicity and infinite wisdom. The answer lies in the twin aspects of death and resurrection. It is only by transitioning (or through transmutation in the dissipation of the physical body) that we may enter the most sublime state beyond death and Union with God. In Rosicrucianism, as stated above, each human being is composed of a physical body, etheric body (vitality) soul and spirit. It is therefore in the presence of death that we rise above it, and the entire purpose of the monument is to inspire this contemplation. The entire construct is therefore about movement, and in this it is most Kabbalistic. The thirty-two (note the correspondence) paths of the Kabbalah are journeys or stages of enlightenment, in which the wit (knowledge) of the aspirant (the "Passenger") is required by him for the acquisition of the Philosopher's Stone (the prima materia/eternal spirit) within.

Beyond its apparent wit, the gravedigger scene in Hamlet conceals many serious reflections on death and resurrection. Hamlet's monologue centres on the gravedigger (representing Adam, the progenitor of death) removing Yorick's skull after an internment of twenty-three years. The scene revolves around the vanity of life and the existential crisis of humanity's painful awareness of death. Shakespeare is essentially writing his own epitaph when Hamlet exclaims:

"I knew him, Horatio, a fellow of infinite jest, of most excellent fancy." *Hamlet* Act V, scene 1

The symbolism of the skull as a metaphor for the passage or movement from life to death and beyond is a powerful one. Although Hamlet muses on the futility that "paths of glory lead to the grave", there are interesting alchemical parallels to be drawn from it (which in turn mirrors the essential message of the monument poem). These are the "base uses [to which] we may return" i.e. returning to the elements when our physical form decays and is no longer inhabited by the etheric body. The synthesis of body, life-force, mind and spirit during its temporal course on earth dissolves, and whatever it is that bridges life and death in organic life departs. Indeed, the hyperbole implies immortality to me, since Yorick lives on! For the alchemists, this generating or vital force was associated with elemental mercury or quick silver, allegorising the substance and nature of man's spirit bridging the dual and opposite, incompatible material body and the substance and nature of the spirit. The absence of this mediating material, the primal material existent in all living things, leads to decay as the body breaks down into its base elements and is recycled.

In Christian esoteric cosmogony, Adam was established by the Creator to be the man-god of the earth, occupying the centre of universal creation from which he was to exercise his powers. At his fall, Adam was precipitated into the terrestrial centre of the physical earth and crawled to its surface. His glorious body was transmuted into a material body of the grosser elements, which became his prison and obstructed all his spiritual faculties. This transmutation of the form of the first man is designated in Scripture by the corporeal nudity of which he was observed and felt shamed. His fall from the celestial centre is indicated by the following words in Genesis 3:23-24:

> "Therefore the Lord God sent him forth from the garden of Eden, to till the ground from whence he was taken. So he drove out the man; and he placed at the east of the Garden of Eden Cherubims, and a flaming sword which turned every way, to keep the way of the tree of life."

Another purpose for the cherubic putti on the monument, therefore, appears to be their role as the guardians of the portal to Heaven. Shakespeare's monument essentially identifies the skull above them with those who achieve a level of enlightenment in the physical world. This is the Man of Desire.[xxix]

It is not known why Shakespeare requested these words to be placed over his nearby grave:

GOOD FREND FOR JESUS SAKE FORBEARE,
TO DIGG THE DUST ENCLOASED HEARE:
BLESTE BE Ye MAN Yt SPARES THES STONES,
AND CURST BE HE Yt MOVES MY BONES.

It is possible Shakespeare never wrote the poem or shared its sentiment, although I suspect it is an allusion to his Catholic belief in physical resurrection, an attempt to throw off too much unwanted attention from grave diggers. The site has not been excavated, merely subjected to ground penetrating radar by archaeologists in 2014, and who reported the likelihood that Shakespeare's skull had been removed by artefact collectors, possibly in the eighteenth century.

As for the skull representing Kether, in a sense it represents the final portal or gateway to harmony and balance, elemental death.

Chapter Eight: Rosicrucianism

Alchemy is comprised of two branches: the practical and philosophical. Practical alchemy was the father of modern chemistry, and concerned itself with the transmutation of matter, in particular attempts to convert base metals into gold or the discovery of an elixir for immortality. The philosophical or esoteric arm of alchemy concerned itself with viewing the elements and metals as allegories for spiritual transformation, and the recovery of the prima materia within humanity and the restoration of our divine state to what it was before Adam's fall. The lesson of esoteric alchemy is essentially on the condition of being, where the Creator's Being is allegorically reflected in the elements, from which sentient life derives its vitality or life force in the form of action, dissolution, and reintegration into new life. This is what is meant by the expression being "made in the image of God."

The fiery water of the immortal Spirit (allegorised as sulphur and salt) has always existed in the centre of man. Mercury is placed in the centre, and between sulphur and salt acts as the vehicle binding those opposites, and is therefore the true centre of the celestial lights. In nature, sulphur and salt are of such contrary types that they can never combine without a reconciling substance. In Trinitarian Christian terms, this is how the incarnation is made possible, and how Christ is both fully God and fully man, and how the Father, ascended Son (the God-Man, Christ) and Holy Spirit are able to co-exist in eternal Unity. This threefold imagery also equates to what the alchemists regarded as the spiritual stages of man: that is, from birth to the age of seven; from the age of seven until death; and from death as we progress through ever subtle and higher worlds. This is the true synthesis of mind, body and spirit, which cannot be fully accomplished during its temporal course on earth. Yet it also proves an "architecture" in the form of humanity, one where our bodies may be likened to a temple, which is the repetition of the general, particular and universal Temple designed by God. There is truly not a grain of earth which is not a temple, since it contains a power, and humanity is the true divine temporal Temple, and it is a matter of rebuilding it.

The Rosicrucians sought initiates whom they regarded as sympathetic to the restoration of humanity's original spiritual memory – what we might call "the collective subconscious" in Jungian terminology. Their doctrine of reintegration equates with the emergence of conscious knowledge from the symbolism inherent in our psyche. When one considers how perfectly this fits in with Jung's doctrine of the collective unconscious, it becomes a powerful self-realisation. They believed that Divinity always dwelt in the centre of man and had never fully departed, despite Adam's prevarication. The Great Work (or *magnum opus*) required for our reintegration with the Divinity was essentially a Quest, and the reason why the Rosicrucians were ceaselessly engaged in the work of the symbolical demolition and reconstruction of their inner natures.

Another way of expressing this, is to say that the Rosicrucians were engaged in the work of retracing a path of return. It was this esoteric alchemical work which motivated such Men of Desire. Yet, we cannot lose sight of the fact that their antecedence preserves the much, much older temple theology of the Jewish Diaspora, understood and applied within an esoteric Christian context during the Middle Ages.

Molded into the arch above the demi-figure are seven red roses. This reminds us of the Rosy Cross of the Rosicrucians, after which the order was named. It originated as a symbol of the sacrifice of Christ and the purity of his blood, or vitality. The red rose is therefore a symbol of purity and of the etheric forces that vitalise our bodies.

In many religious systems the number seven represents the completion of creation. The ancients looked to the natural world and saw evidence of a divine code in the seven colours of the rainbow, seven days of the week and the seven classical planets. The seven planets or "luminaries" were an important part of Sumerian and Babylonian astrology, being those most easily seen with the naked eye. These were the Moon, Mercury, Venus, the Sun, Mars, Jupiter and Saturn. The ancient Egyptians believed each of these spheres influenced the assaying of metals: the Sun, gold; Saturn, lead; Jupiter, tin; Mars, iron; Venus, copper; Mercury, quicksilver; and the Moon, silver. Esoteric alchemy in turn applied the assaying of these metals to the quest for perfection in the development of seven personal virtues, namely: of truth, justice, balance, order, love, harmony and reciprocity. The Pythagoreans regarded the number seven as 'perfect' because it contained the number three representing the triangle, and four, the square, geometrical forms which, when merged, were held to be indivisible.

One Rosicrucian secret is that our physical bodies have a further six nonphysical forms, each of which creates that 'beneath' it. So, when we die certain of these forms perish but the immortal parts do not. There is only one individuality but this is concealed by these seven veils, which are the ever more subtle versions of the self. The seven roses above Shakespeare's head on the monument refer to this Rosicrucian doctrine of the Seven Aphorisms or Sevenfold Soul. These are the elemental, mineral, plant, animal, human, spiritual and divine souls. These equate to the physical or elemental forms found in the mineral, vegetative and animal aspects of our bodies; to consciousness; the mind; the ego; and the spirit. That the seven roses in the monument arch are symbolic of the Seven Aphorisms is beyond doubt. They may also point to the three spiritual stages of man mentioned above.

I do not intend to dwell on the original use of colour in the monument, but it is believed the figure of Shakespeare was once painted in overtly alchemical colours. For instance, his doublet is believed to have been a bright, scarlet red, his gown black, the page of paper white and the cushion green. If so, then each of the four classical elements is represented. Of course, red doublets also represent the arts, and black gowns were worn by intellectuals and divines, so there is a dual meaning.

Was Shakespeare himself a member of an esoteric order or fraternity? Michael White's paper entitled *The Esoteric Shakespeare* is interesting as it casts a light on the popularity and influence of the occult on the intelligentsia of renaissance London. As White says:

> "Two great Renaissance thinkers of the day, Giordano Bruno and John Dee, were both living there. Bruno was in exile from Italy, and Dee, who had one of the largest libraries of esoteric works in his day, was an advisor to the queen. Both had immense influence in the London of the 1580s, just when Shakespeare was making his name."[xxx]

We already know that Shakespeare's friend Leonard Digges' father was educated in John Dee's household. White however provides a detailed look at how these influences materialise in Shakespeare's writing, and two points of particular note sprang out at me. The first was White's observation that In *Love's Labour's Lost* the three principal characters withdraw from society for three years in the pursuit of wisdom.[xxxi] Are these not templates for the references to the wisdom of Nestor, Socrates and Virgil? Nestor left his kingdom for Troy to help Agamemnon; Socrates refused to escape prison and confronted his judicial murder out of strength, and the conviction of his principles; and the Virgil of the *Divina*

Comedia displays all the virtues of the perfected Roman nobleman. These characters are, in short, metaphors of wisdom and courtly love developed beyond the self. Adam White argues that Shakespeare was influenced by his contemporary Catholic mystic and Hermetic occultist Giordano Bruno (1548-1600):

> "Bruno's book The Heroic Frenzies, published 1585, portrayed love as a mystical state that was literally the presence of the divine. Love, for Bruno, was the prima materia, the basic energy of the universe that powered the sun and filled the empty space. It was the vital substance, the ground from which all things sprang. Bruno called love the magnetic, innocent, amoral, primordial nature inherent in all things. The character Berowne in *Love's Labour's Lost* was modelled on Bruno."[xxxii]

White also identifies Bruno's influence in Shakespeare's *Troilus and Cressida*:

> "Ulysses gives his speech about the order of the cosmos and how it relates to the social order of society and the psychological make-up of each person. The most basic principle of Egyptian esotericism, taken from the Emerald Tablets of Hermes Trismegistus, states, 'As above, so below.' This principle, expounded by Bruno, was the founding tenet of Renaissance astrology, which saw the heavens as a macrocosm that determined the destiny of the nations of earth and of people individually."[xxxiii]

This cosmological parity or balance is the key to understanding Shakespeare's monument. It is, in truth, a Rosicrucian memorial. It also underlines the possibility – as yet unproved – that Shakespeare was a member of an early form of speculative Freemasonry. How this might come about when English Freemasonry was not understood to have existed prior to the formation of the first Grand Lodge in London 1717 is the moot point. Indeed, no minutes were taken until 1723. In all probability the answer lies within the context of the economic turmoil caused by the English Reformation, when the operative masonic guilds were forced to depart from working on the grand ecclesiastical structures commissioned by the Catholic Church and had to adapt to smaller, less frequent and secular commissions. Thus, the operative masonic guilds – once Catholic – were inevitably shedding members and morphed into non-religious lodges that gradually accepted non-operative members into hidden, esoteric side-orders. Why these new speculative masons were drawn to the declining operative masonic guilds is explained by virtue of the mathematical and geometrical knowledge the lodges could impart, and hence how masonic guilds were infiltrated by Rosicrucian concepts brought in by the newcomers. Prior to the Reformation, apprentice stonemasons had to study and solve geometrical problems over a three-year period. Given the influence of Pythagorean concepts, and the high status that master stonemasons were held as architects with working knowledge of "sacred geometry", it comes as no surprise that by the early seventeenth century it was fashionable for "gentlemen" of learning to seek to gain knowledge by joining their ranks on a non-operative basis. Bear in mind also that the Rosicrucians sought to use ancient science to design a new world order and saw in architecture a way of furthering this knowledge. We need only consider the trowel and spear in the monument, and the three Working Tools of the Poet in the frieze (the quill pen, page and cushion he needed to sit on while working) to recognise quasi-Freemasonic symbolism. It is therefore not only likely but highly probable that Shakespeare joined an operative masonic lodge taking in new, non-operative members. This was certainly not modern Freemasonry as we know it today, but it was esoteric stonemasonry or architecture nonetheless.

Browning argues that it is no coincidence that in the earliest records of non-operatives being admitted into the London Masons' Guild, since it contained an affiliate society called "The Acception,"[xxxiv] The non-operative members of this highly esoteric order hidden within operative masonry were known as "Accepted Masons." Browning adds:

> "As a result, we see men like the antiquarian Elias Ashmole ... being initiated into Freemasonry. Ashmole was initiated in 1646, but there were many others like him before that."[xxxv]

The *Encyclopaedia Masonica* simply states:

> "The Masons Company of London show this phrase ["the Acception"] in one of their records, 1620-1, in connection with a seemingly non-operative or speculative body which was associated with them. In 1682 Elias Ashmole visited this Lodge."[xxxvi]

Concluding Remarks

I made the decision in this present work to simply highlight the key occult symbolism in Shakespeare's monument. Hence, I have not written discrete chapters on Hermeticism and magic, and must leave it to the reader to discover the beauty, wisdom and strength inherent in their own research.

By way of general concluding remarks on the preceding chapters, it can be said that the monument is a metaphor for an early form of non-operative masonry. It is certainly Rosicrucian, even if the fraternity was comparatively new to England at the time of Shakespeare's death. Certainly, the inferred references to Plato convey Rosicrucian ideals. In his final and most esoteric play, *The Tempest*, Shakespeare introduces Hermetic themes, and indeed the core principle of Rosicrucianism - free-will and free-thought – triumphs in the final act of Prospero when he buries his wand and renounces theurgy.

The monument also undoubtedly incorporates Kabbalistic symbolism. Given that the Rosicrucians, the alchemists and other occultists infiltrated the operative masonic guilds, it should come as no surprise that we can identify overtly Freemasonic symbolism within it. Yet Freemasonry, Rosicrucianism and alchemy have no prior claim on the symbology of death/resurrection, duality and the movement of transformation. These are far more ancient themes which hark back to the core, spiritual memory of our species. They do, however, share many of the correspondences outlined in this book.

No esoteric trend begins in a social vacuum because it takes time to evolve and develop. Freemasonry, alchemy and Rosicrucianism are no exception to this rule. Masonry did not begin with a "bang" in 1717, as we know from the activities of Elias Ashmole, but likewise what existed prior to that point did not constitute "Freemasonry" either. The same can be said of the Rosicrucians, who did not suddenly come into existence in the early 1600s, but became fashionable around that time, when enthusiasts began publishing their ideas. That the monument contains symbols, geometric signs and ciphers is beyond doubt. The question is what, exactly, these allude to if not the earthly incarnation of William Shakespeare? In my opinion the monument is a Kabbalistic allegory set in stone, like the perfect ashlar in Craft Freemasonry.

The themes of duality, physical dissolution and the transformation of man's eternal nature are present. The monument describes that journey in a clearly Kabbalistic fashion, and points to the figure of Shakespeare in the centre as an example of the Middle Way, the sacred path. Why else would Envious Death be covetous of him whom it placed within, but for the fact that Shakespeare has been separated from his physical body and attained eternal splendor?

That we know his monument was not costly reflects his chivalric notions of humility and proportion. The living art on this plane is in the continuance of the performance of his plays, and the influence of his thought on those left behind, who read the magnificent verses on the human condition. The master can no longer write, no longer create in this world, and so we must content ourselves with these as his memorial – the true memorial to his wit and intellect – not stone.
I cannot see any other more satisfying explanation for the poem, which, if the monument is a form of the *Etz Eyim,* serves as a cipher for the journey from the lowest

sephirot of Malkuth (the world of this ordinary life) to that of Kether, beyond. Again, this makes perfect sense of the cryptic Latin and English verses alike, which are a play on the Kabbalistic correspondence of mortal earth and immortal Heaven, symbolised no better than by the carved skull crowning the entablature. This is what it means to be buried in earth and possessed of Olympus.

If we can accept the correspondences, then the monument can be read as a metaphor of the Kabbalistic Tree of Life. Whatever Shakespeare's wishes, or indeed those of his family, it is clear that his friends desired to preserve his link with the occult in his memorial.

Selected Bibliography

Browning, K., *Shakespeare Reinvented.* 2016
https://shakespearereinvented.wordpress.com/2012/
12/16/shakespeare-re-invented-14-to-epilogue/

Dawkins, P., *The Stratford Shakespeare Monument: The Symbolism, Mystery and Secret Message of the Shakespeare Monument in Holy Trinity Church, Stratford-upon-Avon, England,* 2018
www.fbrt.org.uk/wpcontent/uploads/2020/06/The_St
ratfordShakespeare_Monument.pdf

Holloway, C.J., *Shakespeare's Stratford Monument.* 1999
www.hollowaypages,com/shakespearemonument.htm

Jones, B.E., *Freemasons' Guide and Compendium*

MacGregor Mathers, S.L., *The Kabbalah Unveiled.* New York, 1912

Osborne, M.R., *The Brazen Serpent: Chaos and Order.* New York, 2021

Smith, C., *The Shakespeare Monument: A Study in Authentication*
www. shakespearemonument.wordpress.com

Steiner, R., *Esoteric Christianity and the Mission of Christian Rosenkreutz,* Rudolf Steiner Press, 2005

Tutt, D., *The Philosopher In Mourning: Plato's Invention of Hell,* 2012 www.danieltutt.com

Waite, A, E,, *The Brotherhood of the Rosy Cross,* London, 1924

Waite, A.E., *Shadows of Life and Thought*, 1938, London

Waite, *A.E., The Pictorial Key to the Tarot*, 1910, London

White, A., *William Shakespeare's Monument.* 2010, Church Monuments Society
https://churchmonumentssociety.org/monument-of-the-month/william-shakespeares-monument

Index

Abel, 56, 69, 88

Acception, The, 102

Aeneid, 31

Aeons, 48

Aleph, 72

Antony and Cleopatra, 32

Bacon, Francis, 18, 19, 81, 83

Binah, 65

Boaz, 59

Brazen Serpent, 68, 85

Brotherhood of the Rosy Cross, 40, 107, 111

Cain, 56, 69, 88

Chesed, 65

Chevalier Ramsey, 54

Christ, 54, 73

Coptic Church, 89

Crusaders, 85

Dante, 31, 82

Dido, 31, 32, 33, 34

Digges, 15, 43, 45

Divina Comedia, 31, 82, 100

Divina Materia, 54

Divine Code, 78, 90

Egypt, 58, 85

Elias Ashmole, 102, 104

Emerald Tablets, 100

Etz Hayim, 67

Fama Fraternitatus, 40

First Cause, 48

Four Worlds, 78

Freemasonry, 5, 19, 83, 101, 102, 103

Freemasons, 50, 107, 111

Geburah, 65, 67

Gematria, 84

Genesis, 78

Geometry, 47, 69

Giordano Bruno, 99, 100

Globe Theatre, 24

God, 58, 60, 62, 68, 70, 78

Gold, 53, 73

Grignion, Charles, 20

Hamlet, 32, 56, 69, 91, 92

Hanged Man, 87

Haselmeyer, Adam, 40

Henry VI Part II, 32

Hermes, 61, 100

Hermes Trismegistus, 100

Hermetica, 61

Hermeticism, 62, 103

Hippocratis Coi Medicorum Omnium, 86

Hiram Abif, 56, 58

Hiram, king of Tyre, 58

Hod, 64, 67

Holy Trinity Church, 11, 15, 18, 107, 111

Inner Guard, 54

Jachin, 59

John, 48

John Dee, 15, 49, 99

Kabballah, 67, 78, 84, 90

Kether, 5, 65, 68, 69, 73, 91, 94
Lamed, 88
lead, 73, 92
Leonard Digges, 13, 15, 99
Limbo, 82
London Masons' Guild, 102
Lucian of Samosata, 89
Macbeth, 32
Malkuth, 64, 90
Mercury, 73
Messiah, 68
Middle-Path, 65, 68
Montaigne, 44, 56
Moses, 68
Nestor, 27, 28, 30, 34, 35, 99
New Place, 16
New Testament, 48
Nezach, 65
Nicodemus, 68
Pantheon, 24
Pasqually, Martinez de, 3
Pillar of Mercy, 68
Pillar of Severity, 68
Pythagoras, 69
Pythagoreans, 70, 71
Renaissance, 99, 100
Revelation, 48, 88, 89
Richard Gaywood, 20
Romeo and Juliet, 32
Rosicrucianism, 8, 46, 91, 103
Rosicrucians, 70

Salt, 73
Seal of Solomon, 74
serpent, 85
silver, 34, 53, 73, 92
Simple Cipher, 81
Socrates, 29, 30, 35, 99
Spear of Destiny, 51, 54
Stratford, 11, 13, 15, 16, 18, 19, 20, 31, 35, 43, 71, 107, 111
Stratford-upon-Avon, 11, 107, 111
Sulphur, 73
Tarot, 87, 108
Tau, 85, 87, 88, 89, 90
Temple at Jerusalem, 58
Merchant of Venice, 32
The Tempest, 32
Thomas Digges, 15
Thoth, 61
Tiferet, 65
Titus Andronicus, 32
Tree of Life, 59, 67, 90
Trinosophia, 3
Trismegistos, 61
Troilus and Cressida, 30, 34, 100
Ulysses, 34, 35, 100
Vau, 72
Virgil, 5, 31, 35, 99
Waite, 87
Wenceslaus Hollar, 20
William Dugdale, 20
Yesod, 64, 90
Yod, 72

References

[i] Keith Browning, *Shakespeare Reinvented,* 2016. See full paper at: *https://shakespearereinvented.wordpress.com/2012/12/16/shakespeare-re-invented-14-to-epilogue/*

[ii] Ibid.

[iii] A putto is a figure depicted as a male child, sometimes winged. The putto came to represent the sacred cherub and omnipresence of God.

[iv] Adam White, *Shakespeare's Monument,* 2010, Church Monuments Society. See full paper at: *https://churchmonumentssociety.org/monument-of-the-month/william-shakespeares-monument*

[v] Craig Smith, *The Shakespeare Monument: A Study in Authentication.* See full paper at: www. shakespearemonument.wordpress.com

[vi] Peter Dawkins, *The Stratford Shakespeare Monument: The Symbolism, Mystery and Secret Message of the Shakespeare Monument in Holy Trinity Church, Stratford-upon-Avon, England.* See full paper published on the Francis Bacon Research Trust website: *www.fbrt.org.uk/wpcontent/uploads/2020/06/The_Stratford_Shakespeare_Monument.pdf*

[vii] Ibid.

[viii] Ibid.

[ix] C. J. Holloway, Shakespeare's Monument, 1999. See full paper at: *www.hollowaypages,com/shakespearemonument.htm*

[x] Op.Cit. Dawkins

[xi] Nestor's palace is located at the mouth of the River Alpheus, which was diverted by Heracles to clean the Augean Stables and water to Apollo's "oxen of the sun."

[xii] Daniel Tutt: *The Philosopher In Mourning: Plato's Invention of Hell*, June 2012. See full paper at: www.danieltutt.com

[xiii] Op. Cit. Browning

[xiv] A E Waite, The Brotherhood of the Rosy Cross, London, 1924, pp.115-116

[xv] Ibid. p. 123

[xvi] Rudolf Steiner *Esoteric Christianity and the Mission of Christian Rosenkreutz*, Rudolf Steiner Press, 2005, p. 62

[xvii] Op.Cit. White

[xvii] Op.Cit. Smith

[xviii] Bernard E. Jones, *Freemasons' Guide and Compendium*, 1950, p.495-496

[xix] I Kings 7:15–22, 41–42; II Kings 25:13, 17; Jeremiah 52:17, 20ff.; II Chronicles 3:15–17; 4:12–13

[xx] Josephus, *Antiquities of the Jews*, Book 8, Chs. 95-98

[xxi] Op.Cit. Dawkins

[xxii] Genesis 5:22-24

[xxiii] The Tree of Life or *Etz Hayim* is a diagram consisting of ten spheres or sephirot symbolizing different archetypes, with twenty-two lines or paths connecting them. The sephirot are often arranged into three columns or pillars.

[xxiv] Op.Cit. Dawkins

[xxv] See my *Brazen Serpent: Chaos and Order*, 2021

[xxvi] Op. Cit. Dawkins: "If we examine these first two lines of the inscription closely, as carved in the stone, we should notice that certain letters are formed larger than the others: namely, I, P, S and M in the first line, and T and O in the second line – six letters in all. The 6th letter in the alphabet is F. If we count the small letters in each of the two lines, the result is 33 for the first line and 33 for the second ... 33 is the well-used Simple Cipher for BACON i.e. B.A.C.O.N. = 1+2+3+14+13=33, using the 24 letter alphabet used at that time. If we add the F to BACON we have the name F BACON ..."

[xxvii] A.E. Waite, *The Pictorial Key to the Tarot*, 1910, London

[xxviii] *The Works of Lucian of Samosata,* Fowler H.W. & Fowler F.G. (Tr.) Oxford, 1905. Vol. 1, p.30.

[xxix] Intriguingly, as an aside, the 2014 archaeological survey by Staffordshire University which scanned the site of Shakespeare's interment in the chancel at Holy Trinity Church, found a disturbance leading them to conclude - with reasonable confidence - that Shakespeare's skull was not there. Was this intentional on the part of the poet, or was his skull stolen? In the last resort it does not matter, since the body had served its purpose, as the monument relays. Yet, for the sake of propriety, Shakespeare did not wish his mortal remains to be disturbed, conscious no doubt of the fate of his son Hamnet, who died in 1596, and who likely lay in an unmarked plague pit.

[xxx] Op.Cit. White

[xxxi] Ibid.

[xxxii] Ibid.

[xxxiii] Ibid.

[xxxiv] Op.Cit. Browning

[xxxv] Op. Cit. Browning

[xxxvi] See *The Encyclopaedia Masonica*
www.universalfreemasonry.org/en/encyclopedia-masonica